ALSO BY LAURA CALDER

French Food at Home

French Taste

Dinner Chez Moi

Paris Express

The Inviting Life

Kitchen Bliss

Musings on Food and Happiness
(With Recipes)

Laura Calder

Published by Simon & Schuster

New York   London   Toronto   Sydney   New Delhi

SIMON &
SCHUSTER
CANADA

Simon & Schuster Canada
A Division of Simon & Schuster, Inc.
166 King Street East, Suite 300
Toronto, Ontario M5A 1J3

This Simon & Schuster Canada edition March 2023

SIMON & SCHUSTER CANADA and colophon are trademarks of Simon & Schuster, Inc.

For information about special discounts for bulk purchases,
please contact Simon & Schuster Special Sales
at 1-800-268-3216 or CustomerService@simonandschuster.ca.

Manufactured in the United States of America

1   3   5   7   9   10   8   6   4   2

Library and Archives Canada Cataloguing in Publication

Title: Kitchen bliss : musings on food and happiness (with recipes) / Laura Calder.
Names: Calder, Laura, author.
Description: Simon & Schuster Canada edition.
Identifiers: Canadiana (print) 20220410402 | Canadiana (ebook) 20220410496
| ISBN 9781982194703 (hardcover) | ISBN 9781982194734 (EPUB)
Subjects: LCSH: Cooking. | LCSH: Housekeeping. | LCGFT: Cookbooks.
Classification: LCC TX714 .C32 2023 | DDC 641.5—dc23

ISBN 978-1-9821-9470-3
ISBN 978-1-9821-9473-4 (ebook)

I dedicate this book
with love and gratitude
to

NONA MacDONALD HEASLIP,

who couldn't cook to save her life,
but in another way saved mine.

Contents

Introduction

A kitchen, however open its layout may be, is essentially a private space. And, like a cocoon, it is also a place of transformation. Most things that enter it don't reemerge in the same state: kernels of corn go in, and out comes an altocumulus bowl of buttery popcorn; a sack of flour crosses the threshold, and out parade golden boules of sourdough bread; a basket of lemons comes knocking . . . and on it goes. And, of course, we, too, can be transformed by our kitchens.

All my life, I've taken refuge in the heart of the home when the going has been tough. Whenever I've felt lonely, or desperate for purpose, or powerless to change my circumstances, the kitchen is where I've been able to shift gears, gather my wits, and, if not find an immediate solution to whatever might be weighing on me, at least escape for a while and restore myself to balance with some order, creativity, and comfort. I feel the same way about coming to a dining table. As soon as people are gathered round, again our focus can turn inwards—towards beauty, companionship, civility—while backs are turned like shields against the chaos of the world outside.

During the years of the COVID-19 pandemic, many of us rediscovered the restorative properties of our kitchens and, by extension, our tables. They were certainly a chief source of happiness for me, and it got me thinking about the many ways throughout my life that the kitchen and table have played this and other roles, acting as my window on the world, my flying carpet, the telescope through which I have examined life, and as my friend.

Kitchen Bliss: Musings on Food and Happiness (With Recipes) pays tribute to these most companionable of domestic spaces. I hope, as we emerge from what have been a rocky few years for all of us, it will serve as a reminder of what reliable havens our kitchens and tables can be when we need them, and of how much pleasure, satisfaction, insight, and even bliss we can find in them.

Happy reading. Happy cooking. Happy dining.

1

Hopeless Kitchens I Have Known

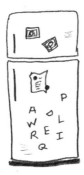

It's a funny thing about me and kitchens. I've never really had a nice one, despite the important place that cooking has always held in my life. Instead, I have made do with whatever has been thrown my way and, though I do fantasize about my dream kitchen (ahem, with separate pantry and scullery), in retrospect I'm rather glad to have been made to understand over the years that the key component to a companionable kitchen is not perfection, but charm. The same, of course, is true of people.

I got a good start at this life lesson, because the rural New Brunswick kitchen I grew up in was about the craziest of the lot. Amongst its many other flaws, it had seven doors, which exited in all directions like a highway interchange. I recently read that the effect of a room is most critically determined by the arrangement of its openings. In other words, if doors and windows are not properly distributed, then no amount of tinkering with a room otherwise can ever make it right.

This must explain why, despite the various attempts to improve it over the years, that kitchen has remained as dysfunctional as ever.

I gave it a good once-over the last time I visited my parents, noting not just the chaos of doors, of which now there are merely six, but all sorts of other idiosyncrasies as well. There's still too little counter space, all of it piled high with things that don't belong together, such as the spot over by a useful plug that contains a toaster, a large sugar crock for baking, an upright roll of paper towel, phone cords, a Kleenex box, tea bags, and a bottle of eyeglass cleaner. The cupboards are scattered at impressive distances from one another, so to assemble a plate, a cookie, a cup of coffee, and a spoon is like running all four bases. Food that you expect to find in the kitchen will often be located elsewhere. Bread, for instance, is on top of a pine dry sink in the dining room, right beside the pottery butter dish with the top from a plastic yoghurt container currently standing in for the lid that got broken. Obviously, the kitchen is too hot for provisions like that to be kept in it, what with the pot-bellied woodstove roaring away on its squat cast-iron legs in the same spot where, in days of yore, the old woodstove for cooking used to be. Above it, high up, hangs a drying beam, which you can lower on a pulley, drape with wet laundry, and squeak back up to the ceiling to dry. Sometimes you'll see a bundle of summer savoury hanging up there, too, tied on upside down to dry not far from a pair of socks. It's worth pointing out that the current incarnation of the kitchen is the result of not just one renovation, but three.

Not that it was without its charms of a less maddening sort, too, mind you. How many kitchens have hanging on their wall a collection of horse brass medallions, including one of the late queen's head, or of lacy, black iron trivets that were once used to set scorching hot sadirons on? (The old models were indeed called sadirons, "sad" referring to how much the things weighed.) There are also two antique, painted, heavy metal models of a "Holstein-Friesian True Type" cow and bull (about eight inches high and a foot long), grazing on a shelf that was formerly a decorative mantlepiece, but that got salvaged by my mother and painted bright, buttercup yellow for the wall above the stove. There's a duck-egg-blue cage the size of a softball that hangs like an ornament from a towel-drying rod and contains kitchen twine, which you access by pulling out the string dangling through the bottom. I could go on, but you get the picture: the whole room was, and remains, a never-ending conversation piece. And it was there, in that kitchen of my childhood—where clothespins were stored next to potato chips and where dinner rolls were shaped and left to rise on a giant breadboard set atop a wooden barrel that otherwise served as a storage space for recycled plastic bags—that I learned the rudimentary principles of how to cook, feed, and eat. These set me up for life. (Organizational skills, I'd like to think, were acquired elsewhere.)

Another highly influential and inadequate kitchen of my life was in the Paris apartment I shared in my thirties with a roommate named Camille. It had no more than two feet of counter space, interrupted by a sink and a tiny gas stove with a defunct temperature gage pressed up cheek-to-cheek with a fridge the size of a suitcase. How we two young women ever fit in there at the same time was nothing short of a miracle, but we did, and not only did we produce feasts for ourselves and our friends in there—coddled eggs with truffle paste, steak au poivre, pasta with bottarga—we could even pull off apéritif (or cocktail) dinatoire for forty. Parties in the latter style could roll on until long past two in the morning, causing the neighbour living beneath us to storm up, bang on our door, and threaten to come back with a gun. We were unfazed, because we'd already decided he was a fool on the grounds that he stank up the stairwell every noon hour with the smell of burnt cheese.

What that kitchen lacked in terms of practicality it made up for in charisma. There was a long shelf above the kitchen sink which housed an army of spice tins sent from a friend living in Kathmandu. We had hooks on the walls for Camille's vintage colanders and my copper pots. Just inside the door was an open cupboard of flea-market dishes—café au lait bowls; bistro plates; tiny, hand-painted juice glasses—and in the corner was a window with a transparent curtain drawn at an angle to one side, like a lock of hair coyly pulled across a youthful brow and tucked behind an ear. Along the ledge, Camille displayed her colourful collection of miniature wooden birds, hoarded from a shop in New York City's Chinatown, and also grew a few herbs. Not an efficient kitchen, perhaps, but certainly one with a lot of personality, which is what counted, along with having a fun, talented, and gung-ho cooking cohort, which Camille was.

But, the dodgiest kitchen I have ever cooked in has to be the one in my friend Nona's garden cottage which my husband, Peter, and I moved into not long before the unforeseen outbreak of the COVID pandemic. It was intended as a temporary measure, but for various reasons, including the pandemic, we ended up staying far longer than expected. The cottage itself was right out of a fairy tale, with a large and handsome main room boasting twelve-foot ceilings, walls covered in fine wood paneling, and forest-green floors. (Once when Peter was on a Zoom call for work, a colleague dryly observed, "I see you've retreated to your Scottish hunting lodge.") From this room, French doors arched by two glorious magnolias led out to an oasis of a garden, bursting with peonies, jasmine, hydrangeas, lilies, and allium. A dream, you say! Yes, but the kitchen in that place, at least when we first moved in, was a nightmare. Its walls were painted a dull, almost dirty beige, and the floors were paved in cold, grey stone. The avocado-hued fridge and electric stove were so old they could have come off the set of *The Brady Bunch*, and the few cheap cupboards, clearly leftovers from another project, had been haphazardly banged into place so that there were gaps here and there that I'd have to find clever ways to fill. Most depressing of all, the kitchen didn't have a window, though there was a skylight high out of reach that let in some light and alerted us whenever it was pouring rain. In retrospect, it was almost symbolic. "This will be a time for looking inwards," the kitchen seemed to portend, unwittingly making the understatement of the century.

Well, I have come to believe that what's outside of us is always a reflection of what's inside, and not liking what I saw, I had to act. I slicked a fresh coat of paint on the walls and hung a chequered curtain over the gap below a counter that stuck out like a missing tooth. A friend put up a thick, wooden shelf along two walls for glasses and dishes, and drilled hooks into another wall for hanging pots and pans. We bought two rattan rugs to warm the floor and installed a knife rack. The large appliances from the Middle Ages were mercifully laid to rest, replaced by spanking new ones. Things were beginning to look up. Then came the final layer: a spice collection, oil bottles, a crock of cooking utensils, a bowl of onions and garlic, another of citrus fruits, colourful hand-woven tea towels, and, of course, our continued, active presence, which turned out to be the biggest energy-changer of all. Over time, we cooked life into that kitchen—Penne alla Vodka, Strawberry Swirl Meringues, Lemon Roasted Chicken—and before we knew it, it had gone from feeling like a prison cell to an artist's atelier. A rescue kitchen, if you will, which, it turns out, when you treat it right, can end up being as lovable, loyal, and life-enhancing as any purebred.

Penne alla Vodka

I don't know what makes the weird alchemy of vodka, tomatoes, and cream so good, but it is so delicious that people can hardly believe their tastebuds. This is a perfect dish to throw together for unexpected drop-ins any season of the year—and, happily, a dish any kitchen can handle.

SERVES 4

2 tablespoons olive oil

1 small onion, minced

2 garlic cloves, grated

½ teaspoon chili pepper flakes

½ cup/125 ml double concentrate tomato paste

¼ cup/60 ml vodka

¾ cup/175 ml heavy cream

Salt and pepper

1 pound/450 g penne pasta

1 tablespoon butter

2 good handfuls of finely grated Parmesan cheese

Basil leaves, torn, for serving

Bring a large pot of water to a boil for the pasta.

Heat the oil in a skillet and gently fry the onion until soft, 5 to 7 minutes. Add the garlic, chili pepper flakes, and tomato paste and cook, stirring occasionally, for about another 3 minutes. Deglaze with the vodka, then immediately add the cream. Season with salt and pepper.

When the pasta water boils, salt it, add the pasta, and cook to just shy of al dente. Reserve 1 cup/250 ml of the pasta water, then drain the pasta. Add the pasta to the sauce along with ¼ cup/60 ml of the pasta water, the butter, and half the cheese. Toss, and continue cooking, adding more pasta water only if needed, until you have a thick, glossy, rust-coloured sauce and the pasta is fully cooked.

Serve with the remaining grated Parmesan and the torn basil leaves scattered over top.

Strawberry Swirl Meringues

The sight of these rose-like confections is something princess dreams are made of, and I promise guests will devour them with the gusto of hungry wolves (not to make them sound like something out of a tale by the brothers Grimm). They have marshmallowy centres and crisp outsides, and they're laced with a small amount of tangy strawberry purée—or raspberry, if you prefer—to offset the sweetness. If you buy a pound/450 g of strawberries, whiz them up with 3 drops of red food colouring, and strain to make 1⅔ cups/400 ml coulis. This is way more than you'll ever need for this recipe (in fact, you'll need only a couple of spoonfuls), but you can freeze it for using in future desserts.

· **MAKES** 16

3 egg whites

¾ cup plus 2 tablespoons/180 g sugar

2 tablespoons icing sugar

½ teaspoon vanilla

2 to 3 tablespoons strawberry coulis (see headnote)

Heat the oven to 275°F/140°C. Line a large baking sheet with parchment.

Beat the egg whites to peaks. Beat in the sugar a spoonful at a time until the egg whites are stiff and glossy. Sift the icing sugar over the top, sprinkle with the vanilla, and fold in with a spatula.

Using two spoons, place 2-tablespoon-sized mounds of meringue, spaced slightly apart, on the baking sheet. Working one meringue at a time, put ½ teaspoon of strawberry coulis on top of each meringue and swirl it in with a toothpick or skewer.

Bake for 35 minutes. Remove from the oven and cool on the sheet for 10 minutes before removing and cooling completely. Store in an airtight container.

2

Cake Lessons

My earliest kitchen memory is of sitting on the counter, wedged in as small as I could make myself, between my mother's mixing bowls and the woodstove. Whenever my mother baked, that sliver of counter was reserved for me and I got plunked down along with teaspoons, the sifter, and all the ingredients, with my legs in hemmed-up hand-me-down red slacks dangling over the flour bags, and my head at the spice rack surrounded by a halo of vanilla, cinnamon, nutmeg, ginger, and cloves. The rest of the kitchen dissolved once my mother started measuring and mixing. I was so preoccupied by the prospect of cake that the entire house could have collapsed and I wouldn't have heard the slightest creak.

My mother's bowl had creamed butter in it, then sugar, followed by the eggs, one by one. She used a handheld electric beater that made swirly ringed patterns around and around in the batter. I always wanted to make rings, too, but I was too small to handle the beaters, so she gave me another bowl with the sifted dry ingredients in it and a pastry blender. I ran that across the dunes of flour and made all the dreamy rings I wanted until she dumped them into the liquids.

Cakes, in our house, were special treats for all occasions, and they existed just this side of the junk-food borderline, so they seemed quite edgy. Any time I caught wind of the fact that a cake was about to be made, I was right there at my mother's shins waiting to be lifted up. These were my first baking lessons. They began when I was two.

On they went, these blissful, buttery, sugary tutorials, until I got old enough to realize that I was being completely ripped off. The shocking revelation came when I started visiting the houses of little friends and was introduced to the superior qualities of the Easy-Bake Oven. Easy-Bake Ovens were doll-sized, made of plastic, and, if memory serves, turquoise. They really worked, too, which amazed me, because they were only supposed to be toys. You plugged them in and the tin-lined oven lit up with a bulb and heated—cooked!—whatever you'd managed to wedge through the slot. I remember one little girl cooked a green bean for me in hers. That was impressive. But it was at another friend's house where I saw what convinced me beyond a shadow of a doubt that I would die a dismal death if I couldn't have an Easy-Bake Oven of my own: cakes, and not just any cakes, either. Easy-Bake Ovens came with teensy round baking tins and miniature cake mixes, including one for pink cakes! I'd never seen anything like them: tiny little-girl cakes, pink as rose petals, pink as cheeks, marvelously, impossibly pink! I went home and fell to my knees. Please! Pretty pleeeease! I'll do the dishes forever. I'll floss every night. I'll sweep!

No.

Actually, what my mother said, specifically, was, "No, you don't need an Easy-Bake Oven. We've got an oven in the kitchen; in fact, we have two and you can use them whenever you want."

Not the same! I wanted to make miniature cakes, and I wanted to make them from mixes. Of course these were the very features of Easy-Bake cookery that my mother was against. What was the use of one, miserly miniature cake? Furthermore, packaged food of any kind was devil-sent in our household. You didn't learn anything by "preparing" packaged food, and anyway the contents of those packaged foods was "cultch!" ("Cultch" was one of our family words, rather onomatopoeic, in retrospect, which meant bad for you and awful tasting, and was applied to anything that came ready-made in a box or tin.) So, that was the end of that. I had to grow up making grown-up cakes in a grown-up kitchen.

One of the first I made on my own was called Never Fail Chocolate Cake with Peanut Butter Icing (from the Baptist ladies' cookbook of Sydney, Nova Scotia, no less). At age six, I entered it in a Loyalist Day baking contest and won first prize. That was the same year I won the hula hoop competition, and my prize was a Coca-Cola can radio and bag of Hostess potato chips. I thought I'd died and gone to heaven.

Another cake I got a lot of practice on was called French Cream Cake, from the book *Out of Old Nova Scotia Kitchens*, which was sort of our Maritime *Joy of Cooking*. I was allowed to make French Cream Cake often because it contained virtually no butter, and because my mother had made it healthier by using stone-ground whole wheat flour in place of white. Right beside where it says "flour" in the recipe, I see there's still a cook's note by little me in brackets specifying "hole whit."

Having spent many years in France since those days, I now look at this recipe and wonder what's French about it. One funny old cookbook I have, published by the Museum of Fine Arts in Boston long before people really started eating "international foods" in America, has a recipe called "Ten Flavor Shrimp" accompanied by a note from the contributor that reads, "I give you something from France." The recipe contains tinned shrimp, garlic, soy sauce, Cognac, and ginger. You're supposed to sprinkle all that with bread crumbs and Parmesan cheese and stick it under the broiler to get bubbly. French Cream Cake is probably just about as French, but the name did serve to glam up the concept of baking it back then.

A third cake sticks out in my memory. I'd told my mother one day that I was in a baking mood and she said I could make Sultana Cake. Well, whatever it was, that sounded like a privilege indeed! So much so, that I thought I'd keep it a secret. Being seven or nine or however old I was, having a secret was pointless unless you could taunt someone else with the fact that you knew something they didn't. So, I went off and found my brothers and, in the best nah-nah voice I could conjure, said, "Betcha don't know what I get to do." Gordon droned, "Let me guess . . . bake a cake." Not to be defeated, I volleyed back, "Yeah, well I bet you don't know what kind!" This sparked the boys' interest somewhat. Then, because I was no better then at keeping my secrets than I am now, I blurted out, "Sultana Cake!" I was imagining a high cake with tiers, perfumed with spices, decked out in princess-frilly frosting, studded with edible beads . . . How jealous my brothers must be!

It turned out to be a white cake with raisins in it. I had to hide my disappointment at how utterly not-at-all-exotic it looked, because I wanted Gordon and Stephen to think I'd been lucky that day. (They couldn't have cared less, but one always likes to imagine being admired for one's every twitch.) I remember how the sound of the name Sultana Cake had sung in my ears in minor key, in raw, faraway vibrations. I saw temples and palaces, urns and strangely feathered birds. I felt the heat of another land's sun, and sands sliding in around my toes, grinding under my sandalled heels. I heard the words of an unknown language scraping and hissing out of the throats of strangers, and I pictured myself wrapped in fruit-and-spice–coloured clothing, my eyes peering mysteriously out of a pale blue veil. Clearly, I'd spent too much time poring over illustrations in Sunday School pamphlets. I've had two encounters with that cake since. Once, for no reason, I was trying to find a recipe for Sultana Cake in a cookbook library. Nearly impossible! Eventually I did find one—one—and that was in an obscure book from Scotland. I thought: Ha! In its hard-to-track-down way, perhaps Sultana Cake is exotic after all, even a bit of a secret. Then, later, on a flight to Marrakech, my dinner tray arrived, and there under a cling-wrap canopy was the ultimate: not just a round of Sultana Cake but in miniature, as if straight out of an Easy-Bake Oven.

French Cream Cake

Using whole wheat flour gives this layer cake an intriguing, earthy flavour, and, as you can see, it contains virtually no butter, so it's light. Note that this cake should be made a day before serving so that the deliberately dry layers of cake have time to absorb the moisture of the pastry cream and the flavours can meld. The result will be soft, moist, and delectable by the time you serve it for dessert or with afternoon tea.

MAKES A TWO-LAYER 9-INCH/23-CM CAKE

FOR THE CAKE

3 eggs

1 cup/200 g sugar

1½ cups/185 g whole wheat flour

2 teaspoons baking powder

3 tablespoons water

FOR THE CREAM FILLING

2 eggs

½ cup/100 g sugar

¼ cup/30 g whole wheat flour

2 cups/500 ml whole milk

1 teaspoon vanilla

1 tablespoon butter

Icing sugar, for dusting

Heat the oven to 350°F/180°C. Grease and line two 9-inch/23-cm layer cake tins.

For the cake, beat the eggs until foamy, add the sugar, and continue beating until thick and tripled in volume, about 8 minutes with electric beaters. Sift together the flour and baking powder, then beat it in, quickly, along with the water, just until combined. Do not overbeat. Divide the batter between the two tins and bake until a toothpick inserted comes out clean, 25 to 30 minutes. Remove from the oven and cool completely.

While the cake bakes, make the filling: Beat together the eggs, sugar, and flour in a heatproof bowl. Scald the milk in a medium saucepan, then gradually whisk it into the egg mixture. Return to the saucepan and cook, stirring over medium heat with a wooden spoon, until very thick, about 10 minutes. Remove from the heat, and stir in the vanilla and butter. Set in a sink of cold water to cool completely. Once the filling is cool, you can also refrigerate it for a short while to firm up even more.

When both cake and filling are cool, split the cake layers in half horizontally. Lay a top layer, cut side up, on a serving plate and spread a third of the filling over it. Lay a bottom layer, cut side up, on top of that and spread with half of what remains. Lay another bottom, cut side up, on top and spread with the remaining filling. Lay on the remaining top layer, cut side down this time. Wrap the cake in plastic and leave it to sit overnight.

Dust the top with icing sugar before serving.

Sultana Cake

I hadn't had a slice of this cake in decades, but last time I visited my parents, there one was on the table, in all its buttery, raisin-studded glory, laced with hints of vanilla, almond, and lemon extracts. With a hot cup of tea, what a dreamy stroll down memory lane.

MAKES ONE 12 × 5-INCH/30 × 12-CM LOAF CAKE

1 cup/225 g butter, at room temperature

2 cups/390 g sugar

3 eggs

3½ cups/435 g flour

1½ teaspoons baking powder

½ teaspoon salt

1 cup/250 ml warm milk

1 teaspoon vanilla extract

1 teaspoon lemon extract

1 teaspoon almond extract

1 pound/450 g sultana raisins

Heat the oven to 325°F/160°C. Grease a long loaf pan, and line the bottom with parchment paper.

Cream the butter, gradually adding the sugar. Beat in the eggs, one at a time. Sift together the flour, baking powder, and salt, then add them alternately with the milk. Stir in the extracts, followed by the raisins.

Pour the batter into the pan, and bake until a toothpick inserted in the centre comes out clean, 1½ to 2 hours. Remove from the oven, and turn out onto a wire rack to cool.

3

A Little Dinner

An unlikely book I found myself settling into during one of the COVID lockdowns was Emily Post's 1922 edition of *Etiquette in Society, in Business, in Politics, and at Home* (a gift from my friend "Charles the Butler," who runs an academy for training household staff). Forbidden from gathering, as we were at the time, I, in a Downton Abbey–esque binge, vicariously lapped up her chapter on formal dinners. It spelled out how the Oldworlds and the Toploftys entertained during the Gilded Age, with their army of servants, arsenal of silver, and tables for sixty. What a frolic! Quelle splendeur! I'd give my eye teeth for that right now, I thought.

But then I turned the page and came upon a small, almost afterthought of a section, hidden somewhere between the etiquette of "withdrawing" and musings on carving (a job best left to the cook, according to the author, unless you're one of "those men"), intriguingly entitled "The Little Dinner." Now what could this be? I wondered. "The little dinner," Post tells her readers, almost in the hushed tone of a whispered secret, "is thought by most people to be the very pleasantest social function there is." What? After all those juicy and glamorous tidbits about balls and banquets, she had something to top them?

Obviously, Emily Post was writing from another era, and from the perspective of a particular class, one that gorged itself on the kind of large, formal, at-home dinners that are all but unheard of today, unless, I suppose, you're a royal. She acknowledged they had their place (even for those who didn't like them, at least as a "spine stiffening exercise"), but she also recognized that a steady diet of them was like sitting down to the social equivalent of a pound of foie gras every night. Ouf! The informal "little dinners," on the other hand, were a chance to relax. They were special because strangers were seldom, or at least only carefully, included, so that intimate conversation was possible. Also, they remained uplifting, because, unlike a simple "supper" (she distinguishes between every possible sort of meal), a "little dinner" was done in exactly the same way as a formal one—the table glamorously set, the food lovely, people dressed for the scene—except that formalities such as being escorted into the dining room in the manner of a state banquet got tossed out the window. (Some people's idea of letting their hair down!)

I was captivated by the appellation "little dinner," because I have practically made a vocation of them my whole life, albeit, in my case they're considerably more low-key. I go through phases where I entertain like a woman possessed (three to four dinner parties a week!), yet I'd never really thought of them as "a thing." Then along came the pandemic, and suddenly I realized what a big deal in fact they are, not just for giving people a break from isolation and the humdrum (the opposite of Emily Post's experience, which was that they gave guests reprieve from being over-peopled and exposed to stuffy entertainments), but also for giving friends a reason to dress up and feel a bit grand and spoiled for a few hours. At the best of times people are pleased to be invited, but during the pandemic, I noticed a kind of gratitude I'd never seen before. People would arrive on our doorstep with grim faces and heavy shoulders, worn down by endless lockdowns and from having to go everywhere in public wearing ugly, suffocating N-95 masks, then after a couple of glasses of wine, a belly warmed by a steaming braise at a properly set table, the lights flicked on in the brain by some lively storytelling and heated debate, they'd leave glowing. "You have no idea what you do," one friend said as she left dinner one night, but I could see with my own eyes something significant was happening. A "little dinner" produced with care can work magic.

UNESCO has what it calls "the representative list of intangible cultural heritage of humanity." On it is the French gastronomic meal, which, when I examine it now, is essentially a "little dinner." It is partly defined by the structure of the meal itself—aperitif, starter, main course, cheese, dessert, and digestif, all accompanied by bread and wine—but also by the meaningful padding around that scaffolding, which includes the selection of dishes and the products that go into them, wine pairing, setting a beautiful table, and gathering around it the right balance of people. And there's more: the concept encompasses the act of appreciating the meal with the brain and all five senses, along with the essential art of conversation. Such a dinner is a serious package, the significance of which the French have long recognized. Perhaps the pandemic helped the rest of us to see the importance of it, too.

Funny how validating it can be when something is given a proper name: A Little Dinner. Sigh. This has always been my hosting sweet spot, but finally having something special to call it felt like being given a talisman. It has forever changed the way I enter the kitchen when I'm about to prepare for a party, which is to say no longer just with a focus on what I can cook to please people, but also with a mission to combat the stress and anxiety that can pixilate the outside world (and sometimes the inside one), pandemic or no pandemic. "Innertaining" would almost be a more apt term than entertaining, when you think of it: intimate gatherings around the table that are less about performing or impressing anyone and more about letting out a deep breath and getting renewed enthusiasm for life by proximity to good food and good people. And that's the irony: there's nothing little about a "little dinner" at all. Frankly, I can hardly think of anything quite as big.

Imperial Cheese Crispies

These are everyone's favourites to go with drinks, so much so that I have a hard time keeping them in the house. If you cannot find dear old MacLaren's Imperial Cheese (the Canadian product that comes in a red and black tub), use any very sharp orange cheddar, grated.

MAKES ABOUT 50

1 package Imperial Cheese (230 g), at room temperature
½ cup/110 g butter, at room temperature
1½ cups/185 g flour
¼ teaspoon salt
⅛ teaspoon cayenne pepper

Cream together the cheese and butter. Stir together the flour, salt, and cayenne pepper with a fork, then add it to the dough, mixing and kneading with your hand until smooth. (This can all be done in a food processor, if you prefer.)

Divide the dough in two and roll each half into a log, about 1 inch/2.5 cm in diameter. Wrap and refrigerate for an hour.

To bake, heat the oven to 400°F/200°C. Line a baking sheet with parchment. Slice the logs into thin rounds and lay them, slightly spaced apart, on the baking sheet. Bake until cooked through and only barely starting to brown, 10 to 12 minutes. Remove from the oven and let cool completely before storing in an airtight container.

Tomato Aspic with Horseradish Sauce

Before you hold up your hands in protest, hear me out. The first time I skeptically tasted this classic was at one of our "Kasserole Klub" dinner parties, the menus for which, according to "klub" rules, must always be built upon retro dishes. I was floored by how good it was, and, frankly, how chic! So naturally I demanded the recipe, which I now produce a couple of times a year, for shock and dazzle purposes, using the San Marzano tomatoes that I break my back canning every autumn. This makes a light and zingy start to dinner that never fails to delight and amuse.

SERVES 8

FOR THE ASPIC

4 cups/1 litre puréed canned tomatoes

1 onion, sliced

1 garlic clove, crushed

1 bay leaf

1 clove

1 teaspoon salt

½ teaspoon finely ground black pepper

2 envelopes gelatine

¼ cup/60 ml cold water

¼ cup/60 ml vodka

1 tablespoon lemon juice

1 tablespoon lime juice

1 teaspoon Worcestershire sauce, plus more to taste

3 dashes Tabasco, plus more to taste

FOR THE HORSERADISH SAUCE

½ cup/125 ml sour cream

2 tablespoons prepared horseradish

Squeeze of lemon juice, to taste

Salt and pepper

Lemon wedges, for serving

To make the aspic, put the tomato purée, onion, garlic, bay leaf, clove, salt, and pepper in a saucepan, bring to a boil, and simmer for 15 minutes.

Five minutes before the tomato mixture has finished cooking, sprinkle the gelatine over the cold water in a large bowl and let stand 5 minutes to soften. Strain the tomato mixture over the gelatine, using a ladle to rub out all the juice through the sieve, then stir to dissolve the gelatine. Add the vodka, lemon juice, lime juice, Worcestershire sauce, and Tabasco, taste the mixture, and adjust the seasonings. Pour into a terrine, loaf pan, or mould. Wrap and refrigerate until set, several hours or overnight.

Meanwhile, to make the horseradish sauce, simply stir together the sour cream, horseradish, and lemon juice in a small bowl. Season with salt and pepper to taste. Refrigerate until ready to serve.

To unmould the aspic, run a knife around the edge of the terrine, dip the bottom in hot water for half a minute, then flip the aspic out onto a board. Smear a tablespoon of horseradish sauce onto each of 8 serving plates. Lay a slice of aspic on top, and serve with an offering of lemon wedges for anyone who wants an extra squeeze.

4

2...4...6...8...

Reading, as I was recently, about the swish dinner parties of nineteenth-century Paris, I was interested to discover that fourteen was considered the ideal number of places to have at a table. (I'm not sure why it wasn't twelve, which I've always had in my head as the standard for a big table, perhaps because cutlery is so often sold in that number.) Apparently, the society of the time was so concerned about making sure no sudden cancellation would reduce a table to the dreaded thirteen (horrors!) that they came up with something called "quatorzièmes"—young men who, though they'd not been invited anywhere, got dressed up for dinner every night of the week all the same, so that if a last-minute call came through asking them to fill in a hole, they'd be ready. How's that for a vocation: professional dinner guest? Or, perhaps what you might call a "table plug."

To have come up with the concept of "fourteens" may sound a bit extreme, but we all know the frustration of having a perfect table planned and then having someone pull out at an hour too late to do anything about it. Worse is to have a guest call up last minute asking if they can bring along an extra, especially when it's a total stranger. Once in Paris I agreed to host a quite large "girls' night" dinner, which included some women I barely knew. One of these arrivistes, clearly raised by wolves in a dense forest, not only called up at the eleventh hour asking to bring a friend that nobody else had ever met, but when I reluctantly agreed she could do so then sprung it on me that it was a man. The evening (along with that woman's reputation in my eyes) was unsalvageable.

The odd-numbers challenge is but one consideration when it comes to table mathematics. Another is being sensitive to the difference that various even numbers can make. I never used to think much about it. I was more concerned about the mix of personalities and the food, figuring, "If two people are coming, why not two more? If six are invited, why not eight?" Well, experience has taught me why: because it won't be the same kind of night. I mean, you can increase the numbers if you want to, but you have to be prepared for the effect your decision will have. I remember two close friends arriving for dinner one evening during the pandemic who, upon spotting another car in the driveway, jerked their necks into their torsos like spooked turtles. "That's someone visiting next door," I explained, which immediately caused their shoulders to drop. "Thank God," they sighed. "We thought we were going to have to be 'on'." There's one example of a case where if I'd thoughtlessly tossed in extra people it would have been a booboo.

I'm not sure that in my younger hosting days I'd have considered a table for four worthy of the dinner party appellation. A "dinner," maybe, but a "party," no. But during the pandemic, what with entertaining suddenly being more-or-less forbidden, a table for four practically felt like a gala. A couple of times a week, we'd choose two guests at a time from inside our "bubble," and sneak them in under the cover of darkness for a little feast. I say "feast," because I suddenly had the urge to put myself out a bit more than I normally would when having just one other couple. Our lives needed elevating, we needed cause for celebration, and we needed something stimulating on the table to get our juices flowing, because the news sure wasn't doing it. As I said to Peter one day on a walk, having overheard the word "vaccine" one too many times, "Even eavesdropping has become a bore!"

"Read not the times; read the eternities," wrote Henry David Thoreau, and it brings to mind the quality of the conversations that took place at our dinners for four. There was nothing superficial about them. People opened up and shared things they'd never breathed a word about before. (You both spent the night in jail wearing fur coats?!?!) We talked about life and ourselves, about the struggles, adventures, and beliefs that made us who we are. This is the beauty of an intimate dinner like that: people let down their guard and get into the nitty-gritty in ways that bond you for life, which is why you save dinners like that for the people you really know well, or hope to.

In numerology, four is the number of stability and solid foundations. No wonder it's dinners for four that are the pillars of social life. Four is also the number of the seasons, the elements, the directions, the phases of the moon, the corners of the earth. The symbolism is as reassuring and grounding as that size of dinner.

As things started to loosen up in the world outside, we made the edgy move of occasionally expanding our table to six. This is the number most people will say is their favourite for the table, and when you sit down and analyse it, you can see why. There's a natural friendliness to a table for six. It's the number to gather when you're craving lighthearted stimulation and some much-needed laughs, yet still want the possibility of maintaining a single conversation at the table.

These qualities fit the bill perfectly for our first pandemic dinner for six, a lunch actually, which was with family, following the death of Peter's father. We sat in the garden, "socially distanced" under a flowering horse chestnut, pouring rosé, reminiscing with laughter, and feeling enormous relief to see everyone in the flesh again. Time had been stopped for so long that suddenly to crank it back to life again for a few hours gave it an illusory quality. Afterwards, we almost wondered if lunch had even taken place. "Life is but a dream . . ." One day we're here, one day we're not. Dine like you mean it while you can.

In mathematics, six is considered a "perfect number," which means it is a positive integer equal to the sum of its proper divisors (i.e., $1 + 2 + 3 = 6$: groovy, what?). This perfection must be why it's a number associated with beauty. And, it's the highest number you can roll on a die. Life may be full of gambles, but six around a table never is.

When at last we braved a table for eight, it was early autumn. Again, we were outside, this time with the barbecue going and with friends from out of town at last back in the fray. We started in the early afternoon and went on all day, the men running back and forth from grill to table, delivering first mussels with cracked pepper, then blistered vegetables and a butterflied leg of lamb. There were salads and grains, a hazelnut cake for dessert, and buckets of wine bottles being popped open as fast as oysters in a shucking competition.

The talk never ceased, what with so many mouths present that had gone slack from insufficient exercise and were keen for a serious workout. As always happens at a table for eight (unless you're saddled with a town crier), the conversation would split apart into fours and twos, then come back together, uniting us all for a spell, before splitting off again into smaller groups. It was the oral equivalent of geese flying south, including the volume. We danced, we were loud, we went late . . . that kind of thing can happen when you get up to eight.

Eight is the number of abundance, not a time for holding back on any element of a feast. It's also the most auspicious number in all of Chinese culture and in many other cultures and religions besides. The shape of the eight is a balanced eternal loop representing infinity, and, yes, in that moment, we wished it could go on forever.

Then came the cold weather again, another surge in COVID cases, and lockdowns that lasted months. Social life returned to being the rare quartet formula (no complaints), but most of the time it was just Peter and me, diner à deux. It becomes interesting when the person you're going to dine with every evening also happens to be the same person you've spent the entire day with in the same room, albeit working at separate tables, ten feet apart. You'd think it would be yawnsville, but, for us anyway, it opened up new possibilities.

The cocktail hour, for a start, took on a whole new relevance. It's one thing to transition from work-a-day life to our off-duty evening selves when there's a commute in between, and another altogether when this is to be achieved without moving an inch. We'd shut the lids on our computers, Peter would shake up a drink, and we'd sit down facing each other without having a clue what we'd talk about. And yet, magically, somehow we'd always have things to say. This was a great lesson: when you want to connect with someone, all you need to do is set your distractions aside and sit down with them. There will always be things to discuss, new ideas to explore, new dreams to unleash, new absurdities to chuckle at. Revived by our tipple, next we'd tie on our aprons and cook together. That's a wonderful thing about a table for two: it's a chance to explore the pleasures of a tandem kitchen as well.

Two reflects partnership. Cooking and dining together certainly became the bedrock of ours. Two is also about dualities: the sun and moon, positive and negative, yin and yang, left and right . . . Opposites balance each other out and shed light on each other, just as the isolation of COVID shone a light on the value of togetherness in every form.

The Last Word

A shaken drink from the authoritative classic cocktails book, *The Office*. Perfect for two writers at the end of a long day.

MAKES 2 COCKTAILS

3 ounces/90 ml gin

1½ ounces/45 ml fresh lime juice, strained

1 ounce/30 ml green Chartreuse

½ ounce/15 ml Luxardo maraschino liqueur

½ ounce/15 ml simple syrup

2 maraschino cherries, for garnish (optional)

Combine the gin, lime juice, Chartreuse, Luxardo, and simple syrup in a cocktail shaker with ice. Shake good and hard, and slightly longer than usual, until chilled and diluted. Strain into two chilled coupes, garnishing with the cherries if you like.

Grilled Mussels with Cracked Pepper

This is a treat a friend of ours makes, and which is easy to scale up or down. It can also be done in the oven on parchment paper at about 475°F/240°C. Have a good pepper grinder on hand for this one, and use a coarse setting to yield nice large flakes of spicy peppercorn.

SERVES 6

3 pounds/1.4 kg small mussels
Freshly cracked pepper

Clean the mussels, pulling off any beard, and pick them over, discarding any that are wide open and tapping any that are slightly open to make sure they close.

Heat the grill to high, lay on the mussels in a single layer, cover, and cook until they open, a matter of minutes, removing the mussels as they do so to a large flat platter (it's important they be in a single layer so they all get pepper). Any mussels that don't open should be discarded.

Season the mussels very liberally with cracked pepper, and serve.

5

Dinner Undone

There's a temporary lift of COVID restrictions right now and my diary informs me that we already have two "dinner debts" to repay this week . . . and now a third couple has just rung up and asked to be invited, so I've penned them in for Wednesday. Turning back a page, I see that we threw three dinner parties last week, too, Wednesday, Friday, and Sunday, plus we hosted a fourth gathering on Thursday for what my neighbour calls "sun-downers." I couldn't bring myself to put out only olives and bar nuts with drinks. Instead, I set out chilled cucumber soup in bistro glasses with a swirl of olive oil and some chopped chives. Then, I produced an herbed frittata cut into wedges so we could eat it with our hands. And finally, Peter carted out a carved-up pizza, which he is becoming quite famous for because he makes the dough and sauce himself and selects choice cheeses and other toppings. So that was the outcome of "come for a drink," but at least it was the easiest party of the week. I threw a cloth over the table in the garden, and plunked down a pretty vase of flowers and a pile of napkins. It looked welcoming, the food was good, the wine was pink and cold, and nobody stayed longer than a couple of hours. I'm now asking myself if I shouldn't be replacing more of my full-fledged dinner parties with alternatives like that apéritif dinatoire (as the French call any cocktail party with substantial enough nibbles to make dinner unnecessary). It might help me survive these phases when demand for at-home entertaining suddenly picks up speed like a carnival ride. Right now, I can barely hang on.

I've had a few good role models in the category of hosts who never make a fuss and who aren't afraid to break ranks when it comes to the traditional dinner party march. For instance, a French friend's signature style is the picnic, which she does all year long, both indoors and out. She buys all sorts of different foods that don't necessarily go together—lentil salad, Asian noodles, fried sausages, poached salmon, coleslaw, whatever appeals to her on the day—then she spreads them all out on the table and invites everyone to dig in at their leisure. It can be slightly chaotic, but sometimes freedom from a perfectly constructed menu that ties everyone to the same course at the same time can be a nice change. If it were me, I'd probably coordinate the food more—bread, cheeses, charcuterie with mustard and pickles, green salad, quiche, radishes with butter—but I suppose that's not necessary all of the time either. And obviously, not every pique-nique has to have a French theme.

For years, our neighbour threw Christmas parties for hundreds at her (admittedly rather large) house, and in place of swarms of insubstantial canapés, the anchoring food offerings were always a large platter of the thinnest possible slices of roast tenderloin of beef along with buns, horseradish, mayonnaise, fried onions, and arugula for DIY sandwiches, plus another platter of smoked salmon with capers and red onion, with rye bread and cream cheese within arm's reach.

Not the world's most ground-breaking foods, you might argue, but they always looked impressive on the buffet, pleased the crowd, and did a fine job of keeping everyone vertical and steady. I'm thinking a similar setup would be a good idea for a Sunday afternoon gathering in the fall sometime, possibly after a brisk group walk. But this is the sort of thing I always say and then never do. I might start off with the intention of serving only those platters, but then I'd panic and add about twenty more, which is surely a form of mental illness. (It reminds me of a retired sea captain I know who confesses, "I have two fears in life: one, that I'll come home and my wife will have changed the locks on the front door; and, two, NOT ENOUGH FOOD!")

Peter and I attended a party a few years ago that left an impression on me, because the host had invited thirty people for dinner—without any help—and wasn't batting an eye. As guests came through her door, they were handed a glass of bubbles (no bothering with cocktail options or other wines, you got what you got). Then, by and by, out came a big bowl of rice, another of shrimp curry, and a salad. We all helped ourselves and ate in our laps, then for dessert she set out a silver pot of hot, strong coffee, a bottle of whisky, and a bowl of whipped cream so we could mix our own Irish coffees. This same woman, leaving a mutual friend's cocktail party another time, spontaneously invited about twelve of us to come over to her house for a supper of scrambled eggs and toast. I offered to pick up a salad on the way and she said, firmly, "No. I said scrambled eggs and toast." We arrived at her house before she did, so we sat on the steps to wait. Eventually, she came down the street nonchalantly carrying a couple of boxes of eggs. Talk about unfazed. I should add that this humble offering was served at a table set as if for dinner at the White House, which made it all the more memorable and hilarious.

What am I getting at? Well, I do love a proper dinner party, obviously, but I'm starting to consider that while the aperitif-plus-three-courses menu formula can be handy to lean on, it's also wise not to become a slave to it. Sometimes we just can't pull it off, especially not night after night after night, without heading for collapse. That evening on the terrace with frittata and pizza gave me a good jolt. What a relief it was to have some of the pressure of yet another dinner party lifted off my shoulders, and I rather think the guests felt the same way.

"'Tis a gift to be simple, 'tis a gift to be free, 'tis a gift to come down where we ought to be . . ." My father has always liked that song, and he must have had simplicity on the brain the other day because he called up out of the blue quoting Leonardo da Vinci. "Simplicity is the ultimate sophistication," he announced. "That's my new mantra." Well, good timing, maybe it should become mine, too. Simplicity can be intimidating, because it has the tendency to bare all, but, surely, it's when we're open in this way that we can most easily connect, and isn't that what getting together with people and breaking bread is all about?

Filet de Boeuf Edmund Gate

I can't tell you what a help an electric carving knife is when you want beef sliced handkerchief thin, which you will for this. Arrange the slices on a platter, surround with buns, mayonnaise, horseradish, fried onions, and arugula, then let people build their own sandwiches. This is also good on a buffet when served with a simple sauce, such as chimichurri, aioli, or pesto. Heads up: the meat wants marinating a day before roasting.

SERVES 8 TO 10

1 filet of beef, trimmed and tied (about 3 pounds/1.4 kg)
⅓ cup/75 ml olive oil
Cloves from a whole head of garlic, peeled
Leaves from 2 to 3 branches of rosemary, roughly chopped
2 to 3 tablespoons Montreal steak spice (this replaces salt)

Beginning the day before you plan to serve the meat, pat the filet dry with paper towel. Whizz the oil, garlic, and rosemary to a paste in a blender or food processor, then massage the mixture all over the meat. Next, rub the Montreal steak spice evenly over, wrap the filet in plastic wrap or place in a sealed bag, and refrigerate overnight.

The next day, remove the meat and set on a rack in a roasting pan. Heat the oven to broil with the rack near the top. Put the meat in, and brown it on all sides, turning every 2 to 3 minutes. (Do not attempt to brown the meat in a frying pan because the marinade will stick to the pan and burn.)

Remove the meat, turn the oven down to 400°F/200°C, and move the oven rack back to the centre. Return the meat to the oven and roast to no more than 125°F/51°C, about 15 minutes. Remove from the oven and cover the meat with foil to rest and finish cooking, at least 20 minutes.

Slice the meat as thin as possible, and arrange on a platter.

Falafel with Tahini Sauce

This recipe was a COVID-era acquisition which I'm thrilled to have in my repertoire because it produces exciting, electric-green falafel that are healthy and packed with flavour, and that everyone (even vegans) can eat. Note that the chickpeas must be soaked overnight before you can make this.

MAKES ABOUT 24

FOR THE FALAFEL

1 cup/150 g dried chickpeas
1 small onion, sliced
1 cup/20 g fresh flat-leaf parsley leaves
1 cup/20 g fresh coriander leaves
1 jalapeño pepper, seeded and sliced
4 garlic cloves, roughly chopped
Zest of 1 lemon
2 teaspoons cumin
1 teaspoon coriander
1 teaspoon salt
Freshly ground pepper
2 tablespoons chickpea or all-purpose flour
½ teaspoon baking soda
Vegetable, canola, grapeseed, or peanut oil, for frying

FOR THE SAUCE

½ cup/125 ml tahini
½ cup/125 ml water, plus more if needed
3 tablespoons lemon or lime juice, plus more to taste
1 to 2 garlic cloves, grated
¾ teaspoon salt, plus more to taste

Continued on the next page

Fresh flat-leaf parsley sprigs
Fresh coriander sprigs

To make the falafel, before you start, the chickpeas must be soaked for 24 hours in plenty of cold water. The next day, drain the chickpeas, rinse in ice-cold water, drain thoroughly, then rub dry with a clean tea towel.

In a food processor, first pulse the onion, parsley, coriander, jalapeño, and garlic, to a coarse meal. Add the lemon zest, cumin, coriander, salt, and pepper, then whizz again to mix through. Add the chickpeas, and alternately pulse and scrape down the sides of the bowl until you've achieved the texture of fine, dry meal. (Do not overwork it to a wet paste.) Add the chickpea flour and baking soda, and pulse a few times to mix through. Refrigerate the mixture for about an hour before cooking. (You can leave it overnight no problem, too.)

To make the sauce, simply whisk the tahini, water, lemon juice, garlic, and salt in a bowl to combine. Add more water, if needed, to thin it to consistency. Taste and correct the seasonings. Transfer to a serving dish.

To cook the falafel, first roll into 24 1-inch/2.5-cm balls. Either use a deep fryer or heat 3 inches/7.5 cm of oil in a saucepan until sizzling (350°F/180°C). Fry the balls in batches, turning occasionally, until all sides are brown, about 3 minutes total. Remove with a slotted spoon to paper towel. Then transfer to a serving dish.

If you'd like a pretty garnish, deep-fry some fresh parsley and coriander sprigs in the hot oil for a few seconds. Remove with a slotted spoon to paper towel. Then scatter over the falafel. Serve with the tahini sauce.

6

My Large Appliance

I have always avoided having any equipment or gadgets in the kitchen (or anywhere else in the house, for that matter) that don't earn their keep. The clutter makes me crazy, for one thing, but I also value my independence too much to get brainwashed into thinking I can't make popcorn without a popping machine or get the flesh out of an avocado without a scoop expressly designed for the task. A few things have crossed the kitchen threshold when my guard was down, but they've not lasted. The InstaPot, for example, was on the curb after only two weeks because I realized that, though it may be useful to a lot of people, I personally didn't need something to make chicken stock in half an hour or cook brown rice in twenty minutes, because I'm home all the time anyway and I can fill in the stretches while things cook with no end of other activities. I had a really slick, jumbo-sized toaster for a while, but that got relegated to the family cottage when I realized that a toaster oven is infinitely more useful and barely takes up more space. As for small jobs, I've always been happy to bash the skin off garlic with the side of a knife, to beat egg whites by hand with a whisk (well, most of the time), and to crush spices in my mighty mortar and pestle. Truly, when it comes to cooking, I'm a bowl and a wooden spoon kind of woman. So, I was a bit taken aback one day, when I looked around the kitchen and realized that a serious accumulation of stuff has begun to take over the countertops.

I will blame this small-appliance pileup on my large appliance, called Peter, who ever since he has been working from home has been occupying increasing space in our kitchen. It began with butter. Someone gave him a book all about how to make it and then next thing he'd borrowed a KitchenAid from a friend. Now he's all the time buying organic cream in bulk and working to perfect his recipe by testing the difference between butter made with a powdered culturing agent versus yoghurt or kefir. I even find myself using the KitchenAid for silly things like oatcakes or cheese biscuits, which is ridiculous because they have so few ingredients in them that a manual approach would suffice. This is how these little dependencies start to creep up on a person, and it's a slippery slope.

A treat of ours, pre-pandemic, used to be going for long, Sunday-afternoon walks and popping into a bar for a refreshing drink on the way home—a flute of bubbles for me, a Manhattan for him—along with a cone of French fries. We hadn't done that in months when it became clear (to someone, anyway) that we desperately needed a deep fryer the size of a dehumidifier so we could make our own frites. It has now taken up residence in a far recess of the kitchen that has to be accessed on hands and knees, an aerobic exercise we take to not just when struck by a craving for steak and fries, but also for falafel and beignets, and by occasional whims to try wonky dishes like corn fritters with deep-fried sage leaves just for the heck of it.

When exactly the ice-cream maker moved in, I cannot say, but the canister for it is permanently taking up half the top shelf of the freezer so it's ever at the ready. I'll admit you cannot beat the taste of fresh ice cream, and ices in general are one of my favourite desserts: salted caramel ice cream, strawberry frozen yoghurt, chocolate sorbet . . . Summer forecasts call for things perhaps blueberry or gin-and-tonic flavoured, while winter weather makes you start to dream of trying recipes like the one for date square ice cream that a friend gave me.

At least a barbecue is of an outdoorsy disposition, so the arrival of the Weber grill (initially procured because Peter wanted to attempt smoking bacon) was something I couldn't really complain about. It lives on the stone patio under the chestnut tree and does, I'll admit, work rather hard all summer. Peter fires it up and produces quite magical things to eat on there: buttery rib eye with a crisp exterior, lemon-saturated chicken suprêmes, a mildly smoked side of salmon, or blistered shishito peppers. I do love the smell of the smoke blowing across the garden, too, and I can't help being impressed by that piece of equipment's ability to draw a chattering crowd as effectively as any office water cooler. As equipment goes, it would probably be faultless if it hadn't been for the fact that it put yet more ideas into Peter's head.

One day he emerged from the butcher carrying a very large box. "What have you got there," I asked him, "a suckling pig?" It turned out to be a supply of Japanese charcoal that is meant to be exquisitely pure (enough so, in fact, to filter water). It comes in perfectly even ten-inch logs with deep, bark-like indentations, and it burns for hours and hours, although this I didn't find out for a couple of weeks because that's how long it took for the heftily priced ceramic Japanese grill, ordered when I wasn't looking, to arrive and finally give that gourmet charcoal an active role in life. It is the size of maybe not a shoebox, but let's say a boot box, designed to sit on a table, which is exactly where it goes, right next to the outdoor dining table, so that Peter can create four-hour tasting lunches with every course involving a different grilled thing. I was worried that the contraption would be a redundancy, but in fact it cooks in a completely different manner from the other barbecue. Scallops seared on it, for example, acquire no grill marks and cook with only the most delicate grill flavour. Skewers of chicken leg meat come off so tender, juicy, and light you can't quite believe what you're eating. Still, I wonder how long that novelty will last before I decide to fill it with dirt and poke in some geraniums.

I thought perhaps the paella pan would at last get put to use by autumn, though not for actual paella. The gizmo arrived from Spain a little too late in the season to enable us to make ski-slope–style tartiflette, one of Peter's ideas for outdoor entertaining during the cold months. Mind you, there's now another looming threat to the paella pan's future, possibly to that of the other equipment, as well. Peter has reminded me that he will one day be called back to work at the office. Then what? I don't know how to operate the deep fryer, I can't light the barbecues, I even still fight with the buttons on the toaster oven. And what does this prove? I'll tell you what it proves: not that I've successfully remained independent of small appliances, but that I've become irreversibly dependent in the kitchen on my large one.

Oven Frites in Beef Tallow

Proper French fries are certainly a treat and, though these are not quite the same, they are nevertheless gourmet, not only because of the flavour lent them by the beef tallow, but because of the two-temperature cooking method (typical for deep-frying, too) which gives them that wonderful dual texture: crisp on the outside and soft inside. I buy beef tallow from my butcher, but if you can't find it, use duck fat (equally good) instead. Obviously, oil, grapeseed or peanut, works as well, though it's less flavourful.

SERVES 4

3 large russet potatoes
¼ cup/60 ml melted beef tallow (or duck fat)
Salt and pepper

Peel and cut the potatoes into long, elegant fries. Soak in cold water for half an hour or longer. Heat the oven to 400°F/200°C.

When the fries have soaked, drain them, and spill onto a clean tea towel. Cover with a second tea towel, and dry thoroughly. Transfer to a bowl and toss with the tallow. Season with salt and pepper, then spread into a single layer on a parchment-lined baking sheet.

Bake the fries until cooked, but still pale, 20 to 25 minutes, depending on size, then crank the oven to 450°F/230°C and continue cooking, tossing once or twice, until the fries are crisp and golden, 15 to 20 minutes more.

Remove from the oven. Taste for salt, and sprinkle over more if needed. Transfer the frites to a serving dish and deliver them to the table swiftly.

Prune and Praline Nougat Glacé

A lovely ice for winter, and fun to make. No ice-cream machine required.

SERVES 8

FOR THE PRALINE

½ cup plus 2 tablespoons/125 g sugar

¼ cup/60 ml water

½ cup/75 g slivered almonds

FOR THE NOUGAT

3 eggs

3 tablespoons sugar, divided

1 cup/250 ml heavy cream, chilled

2 tablespoons Armagnac

4 ounces/125 g pitted prunes, chopped

Lay a sheet of parchment paper on a baking sheet and grease it. Place a bowl in the freezer to chill for whipping the cream. Line a 9 × 5-inch/23 × 12-cm loaf pan with plastic wrap.

For the praline, put the sugar in a saucepan, pour the water around the edges, then heat to dissolve, and cook, without stirring, but with occasional swirling of the pan once it's liquid, until the syrup turns to golden caramel. (Don't let it get too dark or it will be bitter.) Stir in the almonds, then pour onto the parchment, tilting the pan so it spreads into a sheet. Allow to set, about 15 minutes, then lift the praline off to a cutting board, and chop into small pieces. Set aside.

For the nougat, separate the eggs: place the whites into a large bowl and slip the yolks into a slightly smaller one. Using electric beaters, first beat the whites to peaks, then beat in a tablespoon of the sugar. Next, plunge the beaters into the yolks, adding the remaining 2 tablespoons of sugar, and beat until thick and pale. Remove the chilled bowl from the freezer, pour in the cream, and beat the cream to thick peaks, adding the Armagnac at the end.

Scatter the chopped praline and prunes evenly over the cream, top with the egg whites, then top that with the yolks. Gently fold all together so that the fruit and nuts are evenly distributed and the cream and egg mixtures are thoroughly combined. Transfer to the prepared pan, wrap tightly with plastic wrap, and freeze for several hours or overnight. Serve in slices or scoop into dessert coupes.

7

Fusional Food

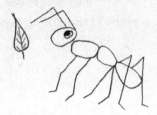

The friend who once accused me of being "bristling with independence" would be shocked to see me now. It used to be that I'd hop on a plane and fly off anywhere alone, even sometimes stay in a strange place for months by myself, but these days I rarely even go to the grocery store unaccompanied by you know who. I used to feel perfectly confident bombing about places like Italy in a rental car; now I get nervous just driving across town by myself because I've become too accustomed to Peter taking the wheel. I haven't booked a restaurant, done my own taxes, taken out the garbage, checked the stock markets, or dealt with a phone company in so long it's embarrassing. Even dinner is starting to make me look incapacitated! I rarely cook meat or fish anymore because Peter is such a dab hand at it, and though I like to think I'm still chef of my own kitchen, since mostly I'm the one who calls the shots when it comes to what we'll be eating, just the other day Peter beat me down and made mussels in cream for a starter, even though I'd been campaigning for plain old moules marinières. So, perhaps even that role is eroding. In any case, it's pretty clear that Little Miss Bristling with Independence has now become half of a couple that yet another friend has declared (not uncritically either) "fusional."

Is it such a bad thing? I do worry sometimes about the truth in the expression "use it or lose it." I don't want to turn into one of those little old ladies who couldn't make sense of a fuse box if her life depended on it. (Ahem, I'm already a youngish lady who can't, so chances are slim.) But I must say that after having cooked by myself for decades, I do love having a companion in the kitchen, even if some of my own skills may be growing slightly dull as a result. It's much more relaxing to have someone else pour the oil over egg yolk and mustard for mayonnaise when you're the one whisking. It's a godsend to be able to ask someone else to take a cake out of the oven for you when you're up to your elbows stuffing cabbage rolls. And, in general, the pressure that evaporates when you know that credit or blame for a meal isn't going to be heaped all onto your shoulders alone is like having a concrete block turn into dandelion seed and float off into the blue yonder on a whimsical June breeze. Besides, it's just plain old more fun to have someone to cook with.

When you think about it, solo cooking probably didn't happen all that often in the old days. Households were multigenerational, so, although men weren't generally anywhere near the stovetop, at least sisters, grandmothers, aunts, and mothers would all have been there together, chattering away while fruits were canned, a harvest of squash put up to freeze, pâtés set in their water baths to simmer away. By contrast, today's world is all about the individual. My phone, your phone; my computer, your computer; my car, your car . . . It has got so that people barely make a pot of coffee anymore, because, instead, it's machines which, one capsule at a time, produce one cup of coffee at a time. My coffee, your coffee . . . You have to wonder if the concept of sharing isn't on the brink of extinction altogether. At least I'm no longer contributing quite as zealously to its demise as I was back in the days of "I can do everything myself!" Perhaps I've finally clued into the reality that, as Mark Twain put it, "To get the full value of joy you must have someone to divide it with."

This may explain why my favourite way to serve food is family style: it reinforces the idea that meals are meant to be communal. It encourages interaction, too, because you have to pass things around so people can get a spoonful of potato gratin or another piece of chicken without dislocating a shoulder or batting a glass of Côtes du Rhône into someone's lap. Even individually "plated" dishes, like crème brûlée or glasses of cold beet soup, look much more impressive when they're delivered to the table all on one large, gracious tray. It always makes me feel a little rebellious to do that, a satisfying little protest against a world that can sometimes seem too intent on keeping us all separate one from another.

You have to wonder if there aren't ants crawling around out there who fancy themselves mavericks. From our towering vantage point, they all look like one unit, a giant machine of many parts operating perfectly in sync as they carry off little wood chips, seeds, and bits of earth. But, you never know, there could be at least one in that tireless marching army of exoskeletons thinking he's the Donald Trump of anthills. "Yup, I built all this!" A self-made ant, in his own mind. Sounds ridiculous, but it's all too easy to think that way ourselves. "I made this dish!" Good for you. But, did you grow the lemon? Did you harvest the vanilla? Did you mill the wheat, pluck the chicken, forge the frying pan, construct the oven? And there you see where food is busy connecting us before it even enters our kitchens, let alone reaches our tables. It links us to farmers, makers, and merchants like a chain of paper dolls. In that sense, food is fusional by nature, so perhaps that's not such a bad word after all. If I appear to have lost my independence in the kitchen, even in life, well, on examination it seems only to have been an illusion anyway.

Salmon with Fennel, Lime, and Sumac

We make this surprising recipe from the Middle Eastern cookbook *Malouf*, by Greg and Lucy Malouf, all the time, and we're grateful not only for how it tastes, but for what it taught us. The toasted lime zest was a revelation, as was the cooking method: that immediate and constant shaking of the pan as you sauté is what's key to preventing fish from sticking. Everyone who eats this asks for the recipe. Serve with a shaved fennel salad dressed with lime juice, salt, and oil, or perhaps with a creamy slaw.

SERVES 4

FOR THE SPICE MIX

1 tablespoon fennel seed

Finely grated zest of 1 lime

1 teaspoon ground sumac

FOR THE SALMON

1¼-pound/560-g slab of salmon, skin on

Salt and pepper

1 tablespoon olive oil

2 teaspoons Dijon mustard

To make the spice mix, heat the oven to 250°F/120°C. Scatter the fennel seeds and lime zest on a baking sheet and toast for 15 minutes. Remove from the oven and grind in a mortar and pestle with the sumac. Set aside.

Move the oven rack to its highest height and turn the oven to 475°F/240°C.

To make the salmon, season the fish with salt and pepper, and heat a heavy, ovenproof frying pan on the stovetop. Add the oil, then lay the fish in, skin side up, and sauté, shaking the pan constantly, for 30 seconds. Turn and sauté the skin side for another 30 seconds, still shaking the pan. Remove the pan from the heat.

Brush the flesh side of the salmon with the mustard, for "glue," then sprinkle the spice mix evenly all over top. Transfer the pan to the oven and cook the fish to your liking, 5 to 7 minutes depending on how well you like it cooked. Transfer to a serving platter.

Lemon Roasted Chicken
with Jus, Frisée, and Dill

Considering how often chickens get roasted around here, you wouldn't think one could ever surprise me, but this result of one night's improvisation was so impressive it had to be written down. What's wonderful about this is the generous amount of jus, which gets poured over both chicken and frisée (curly endive) to dress them. Know that this is a fine recipe also for a couple of Guinea hens, though in that case the roasting time will obviously be shorter. Sweet potatoes, popped in the oven halfway through roasting the chicken, make a perfect accompaniment (see instructions below).

SERVES 4

1 small chicken, about 3 pounds/1.4 kg

Salt and pepper

A few sprigs of thyme

½ lemon, quartered

4 tablespoons butter (2 softened, 2 cold and cut into pieces)

⅓ cup/75 ml white wine

½ cup/125 ml chicken stock

4 generous handfuls of frisée (about 1 medium head), trimmed

A handful of chopped fresh dill

Olive oil

If you can leave the chicken unwrapped in the refrigerator overnight, do so, to dry out the skin. Otherwise, pat it dry, and season inside and out with salt and pepper. Poke the thyme and lemon into the cavity, then truss the bird, rub all over with the soft butter, and set it in a baking pan.

Heat the oven to 400°F/200°C.

Roast the chicken, basting occasionally, until the leg juices run clear, about an hour and 10 minutes total. (Alternatively, a thermometer inserted in the leg should measure about 165°F/74°C.) If the bird is not fully cooked (and if it's bigger, it won't be), continue roasting until done, between 5 and 15 minutes more, depending on size. Check for doneness, then remove the bird from the oven and transfer it to a cutting board to rest for a good 15 minutes while you prepare the jus.

If there is excess fat in the pan, pour some off. (You can freeze it for adding to rice sometime.) If it's just a bit, leave it. Deglaze the pan with the wine, then pour into a saucepan. Bring to a boil and add the stock, then continue boiling to reduce by half, about 10 minutes. Remove from the heat, and whisk in the cold butter, a piece at a time. Taste, and season with salt and pepper.

Carve the bird, in the classic manner, into 8 pieces. Arrange the frisée, scattered with dill, on a serving platter. Season with salt and pepper, and drizzle with a little olive oil. Arrange the chicken pieces on top, pour the pan juices over, and serve.

Roasted Sweet Potatoes

Peel and cut 2 large sweet potatoes into wedges, spread them on a baking sheet, drizzle with olive oil, dot with butter, and season with salt and pepper. Put them in the oven on a rack beneath the chicken 20 minutes before it's done, then when the bird comes out and is resting, raise them up to the higher rack and continue roasting until tender and crispening at the edges, about 15 minutes longer, depending on the size of the wedges.

8

Ageless Appetites

There was something quaint about my father's outrage, though he was quite right. It was towards the end of June and he had been to visit a friend living in one of those "long-term care homes." They'd had lunch and exchanged news, the most devastating piece of which was—and I know this because it was passed on to me in a tone of disbelief—that throughout the entire spring, my father's friend had not been served a single strawberry. "No fresh strawberries!" my father wailed in indignation. "It's criminal!"

Ah, brave new world. Only people with a certain connection to the earth (gardeners, gourmets, and farmer's-market afficionados) seem to have any sense of seasonality when it comes to food these days, with the exception of the "pumpkin spice latté" consumers who get jolted into awareness that autumn has arrived thanks to all the coffee shops putting the drink back on their menus. Otherwise, the food industry—especially when it comes to food in institutions such as hospitals or "homes"—largely turns a blind eye. If you're sick or old, whether it be January or July, it's fishcakes and applesauce for you. (This could be said about the way that children are generally fed, too, come to think of it.)

My parents cannot get their heads around this. They grew up in a time and a place where when local produce was in season you ate it until you couldn't bear so much as to look at another zucchini, blueberry, or cob of corn. Even when I was growing up, we gorged on every glut of lettuce, peas, and asparagus—and ate little else—until Jack Frost put his finger to the garden's lips for another year. The idea of living through any fruit or vegetable's peak without eating it was unheard of.

Old people are misunderstood on many counts, and not least of all when it comes to what and how they like to eat. It's mostly assumed that they don't really care about eating at all, hence all the chicken and frozen peas under bland kerchiefs of béchamel and the stewed prunes in saucers. If that were the kind of offering placed under my nose on a daily basis, surely my interest in food would swiftly vanish, too.

What I lack in the experience of feeding children, I have more than gained in feeding the elderly over the years. I have a number of friends in their eighties and even in their nineties, as it happens. Perhaps I'm comfortable with them because I was brought up surrounded by grandparents, great-aunts and great-uncles galore, and countless neighbours with names like Vida, Zetta, and Clem. I grew up knowing how to treat them: i.e., exactly the way you'd treat anybody else.

Mind you, I was, and am, aware that old people have a certain superior status. Whenever my grandmother came to visit, we children had to stay out of "Grammy's chair," and the old lady up the road with the poodles we were to address as "Miss Newcomb." (We obliged as best we could: "Snookum.") We knew that, physically, old people were a bit different from us, too. For instance, on the way to Vida's house once, we were told we had to speak up because she was deaf. As soon as we were through the door, we raced over to her and demanded confirmation at the top of our lungs: "VIDA! ARE YOU DEATH? ARE YOU DEATH?!" Otherwise, old people were just plain normal, including by virtue of the fact that they liked to eat.

My grandparents used to love coming to dinner at our house from their apartment upstairs, because I routinely turned their visits into an excuse for a dinner party. No mac and cheese on a night like that. I'd pull out the cookbooks and attempt grand-sounding dishes such as Country Captain and Chocolate Torte Royale. I never saw them take any bird-like portions, either. These days, I have a whole list of people considerably older than me who come to dinner in regular rotation. I don't know how most of them eat when they're alone, but they sure tuck in at our place. One loves lamb navarin, another vitello tonnato, one relishes beets in any form, and another, who doesn't even like dessert, once reached for a second helping of baked bananas in coconut cream. On top of that, some of the liveliest conversations you could ever hope for take place over those little dinners.

What isn't any fun, and this is true at any age, is cooking and dining solo day after day. That may be the explanation for old people's presumed fondness for grocery store potato salad and tinned baked beans. Given an alternative, however—new potatoes from the farmer's market with yellow beans, a scallop of delicate salmon in a pool of sorrel sauce—believe me, they'll leap on it every time. It makes them feel alive and loved. I know, because they've told me. It makes anybody feel alive and loved, for heaven's sake! That and being part of dinner-party gossip and debate makes people shed years, both in their own minds and in the eyes of anyone younger at the table. Old people, it turns out, have jealousies, get mad, fall in love, have opinions, have made the same stupid mistakes the rest of us are still busy making. And sometimes they even swear. Who knew?

Well, not everyone operating "care homes," it seems. One of my grandmothers had to be in a place like that towards the end, and, following a car accident, my grandfather had to take a long taxi drive into the city every day to visit her. One time, desperate for a nap, he lay down on the bed beside her and put his arms around her. The nurses raced in tut-tutting "None of that!" and he was swiftly shooed out and into a hard chair. My grandparents, at that stage, had been married for sixty years.

Forgive them for they know not what they do. Well, one day those insensitive types who seem to have forgotten that old people are human will get their comeuppance: the day no mirror recognizes their own face anymore, when their legs won't obey commands to dance, and when some all-knowing young entrepreneur, who has decided that obviously old people couldn't care less about what they eat or how, sets before them, one strawberry-sunny day in June, a microwaved hash brown and a saucer of tapioca pudding.

Baked Bananas with Coconut Cream

Banal bananas, perhaps think you, but I am telling you people love these. It's one of the world's simplest desserts, terrific to pull out of your hat when guests land at short notice, and also one of the most comforting. For whatever reason, their deliciousness comes as a surprise.

SERVES 4 TO 6

4 firm, ripe bananas, peeled and halved lengthwise

4 tablespoons melted butter

4 tablespoons brown sugar

A sprinkling of rum (about 2 tablespoons)

½ cup/125 ml heavy cream

2 teaspoons sugar

½ cup/50 g shredded, sweetened coconut

½ teaspoon kirsch

Heat the oven to 375°F/190°C.

Arrange the banana halves in a greased, shallow baking dish, brush with the melted butter, sprinkle over the brown sugar, and drizzle with rum. Place in the oven until the bananas are soft and the sugar has melted, about 15 minutes.

While the bananas bake, whip with cream to soft peaks, then beat in the sugar. Fold through the coconut and kirsch. Pass separately in a bowl to accompany the bananas, warm from the oven.

Smoked Salmon Terrine

Sometimes showing care through food isn't so much about what you serve, but how you serve it. Of course, you can put some smoked salmon on a plate, scatter over some capers, and slide it under someone's nose, but you can also layer it up with garnishes in a terrine to make an absolute showstopper of a dish. This is adapted from a recipe by the late Gary Rhodes, and I've been making it for celebrations for years. It's quick, it's as easy as anything to make (though you must make it a day before serving), and it has I-care-about-you written all over it. Serve with a garnish of lightly dressed watercress or lamb's lettuce. Thin rye crackers are also a nice accompaniment.

SERVES 16

¾ cup/170 g unsalted butter, softened

2 ounces/50 g marinated anchovies, mashed

Zest of 1 lemon

Juice of ½ lemon

2 tablespoons chopped fresh dill

Pepper

2 pounds/1 kg sliced cold-smoked salmon

Line a 4 cup/1-litre terrine with plastic wrap. Make a spread by mixing the butter, anchovies, lemon zest and juice, and dill. Season with pepper.

Line the terrine widthwise with the salmon, using large pieces that will hang over the edge of the terrine for folding in at the end. Spread the base with a thin layer of the butter spread, then lay in a layer of salmon. Continue in this way until all the fish and spread have been used. Fold the overhang to cover the top.

Cover with plastic wrap, then cut a sturdy piece of cardboard to fit inside the top of the terrine and wrap the cardboard in foil. Lay the foil "lid" on top of the terrine, then place two heavy tins on top to weight it. Refrigerate overnight.

To serve, remove the weights and the foil lid. Unmould the terrine. Slice with the plastic still on, then peel away the plastic and place each slice on a serving plate.

9

Right Table, Wrong Time

In my early twenties, I flew to India with a girlfriend to backpack around the country. We had visas to stay six months and had already been on the road for about three weeks—from Delhi north to Shimla and Dharamshala, back down and west to Jaipur and Jodhpur—when we had what I still consider to be one of the strangest meals of my life. I don't remember where we were, perhaps in Pushkar, famous for its annual camel fair, because at around the same time we went on camel safari overnight in the desert . . . Anyway, we were staying in a cheap hotel (it cost something like fifty cents a night), having told ourselves that we wanted to live like the locals while we were in India, whatever we thought that meant.

The day of the camel safari we didn't eat anything, apart from a pineapple I'd brought along just in case. It had been a long day riding under the searing desert sun and our backs were killing us from the constant thrusts caused by the camel's gait. Also, my travelling companion had a severe case of what we tourists referred to as "Delhi belly," which meant she'd been up and down off her camel every time we came upon a shrub sizeable enough to act as a shield from our guide. (I turned out to have a stomach of steel, myself, perhaps owing to all the unpasteurized milk of my youth.)

We were ravenous by the time we stopped riding to build a camp for the night under the stars. Our guide told us he would cook our meal, and we watched with wonder as he built a fire out of camel dung, slapping it between his hands into patty fuel. Once the fire was going, he took a ball of dough from one of his packs and slapped it likewise to make flatbreads—between those same two (unwashed) hands! That did it for two squeamish young women from cellophane-wrapped Canada. It was terribly rude, but we didn't touch those camel-dung breads or anything else he made, just my pineapple. That was a strange meal, too, but not as strange as the one that came on its heels.

Next night, back at our hotel, I noticed a sign on a bulletin board. "Spiritual Meal, 6 P.M., all welcome." It was being offered by a religious group, which made me slightly hesitant, not really understanding what it was all about, but I had heard they were known for their fabulous cuisine, and not having had a proper meal in nearly two days, I pleaded with my friend that we should go. "It might be the best food we eat this whole trip!" I stressed. "And, it's free!" It took all day to convince her, but at last, her Delhi belly having subsided, she caved. So, at the appointed hour, we trotted around to the back of the hotel where the hosting group had set up tents and outdoor carpets strewn with pillows, along with a large screen, perhaps for a post-feast movie. We sat down in a horseshoe and got comfortable, awaiting the long-anticipated delivery of rice, spicy kabobs, rich dal, samosas, chapati, vegetable stews, and whatever else might surprise us. We waited. Nothing was coming, yet. We waited some more. A few stragglers came along and joined the horseshoe, and at last, a leader welcomed us to the spiritual meal and began by telling us about the glories of the religious group, which he, a shaved-headed blond with a slight German accent, had joined not all that long ago. When at last he'd finished telling us tales about his new and improved life since joining the tribe, we clapped and looked around, anticipating the long-awaited parade of culinary delights to be delivered around, perhaps exotically on bananas leaves. Nope. He pressed a button somewhere and on came what would be a two-hour documentary about an enormous new temple being built by the group—a lot of white and gold, I seem to remember—for which they were raising funds.

By now, I was starting to panic, and it didn't help that my friend had started to hiss at me. "Let's go!" she pressed. "The restaurant will still be open. We can get something there." "Just let's wait a little longer," I held out. "It's sure to be coming soon." To make a long story short, for "dessert" there was drumming and chanting. After another victual-free hour of that, even I finally gave up.

As we skidded into the hotel dining room, by now nearly empty, we thanked our lucky stars that it was indeed still open, because by now it was our stomachs doing the chanting. Against a wall, under fluorescent lights, there were long tables covered in a row of promising chafing dishes and we studied the menu for only a few voracious seconds, before pushing back our chairs ready to get up and dive in. Then, suddenly, something caught the corner of my eye: shooting along the tabletop under the silvery-legged dishes was a mouse, gunning it for the crumbs of who knows what at the far end. Honestly, if the gods had wanted me to fast, why didn't they just say so? We fled the dining room and went to bed hungry once again. Next day, we packed our bags and flew about 2,500 kilometres south, hoping for a change of luck.

I presume that by now Kovalam Beach in Kerala is built up, but back then, it had only one or two proper hotels, mostly high up in the hills, and otherwise consisted of a jumble of colourful shacks serving as motels and open-air restaurants along empty stretches of white sand. We decided this would be a good place to recover from some of the more trying aspects of our journey before heading back up around the other side of the country, so we got a room in one of the hotels on the beach and settled in for a couple of weeks of leisure. It was a bit like being in India without really being in India, because apart from getting yoga lessons twice a day, we barely engaged with the place. For the most part, we lay on the beach reading cheap paperbacks from a bookshop called Brothers Tailor, the only interruptions coming from a lady selling mangos and papayas from a basket on her head and from a man in a tan suit with a voice like Michael Jackson who went up and down the beach in a slow, cool saunter, presenting his portable display of dark glasses while cooing the word "Sunglass?"

One day at Brothers Tailor, I made the mistake of plucking *A Year in Provence* by Peter Mayle off the shelves. I'm still in possession of the tattered copy that broke this camel's back. As my body lay on the beach, turning its pages, my mind flew off to the other side of the world where it drank wine, slathered pâté on baguette, and sank its teeth into lemon tarts. That did it. We immediately booked tickets home (I have no doubt India was glad to see the back of us), and I began plotting my way to France. I'm rather ashamed to admit to all this, but in retrospect I can clearly see that I had no business being in India at that age. I was too immature, inexperienced, and naïve to take in what the country had to offer, a horse led to water that had no idea how to drink.

I bring this up because for the past year—which is decades on— out of the blue I've suddenly found myself gravitating towards things Indian. I watch YouTube videos of the motorcycle-riding mystic

Sadhguru. I've ditched Western yoga and taken up classical Hatha yoga with Indian teachers. I've taken online courses through a couple of ashrams about nutrition and the Indian equivalent of feng shui. I've been encountering Indian perspectives on food and life that are finally giving me a glimpse into the culture that so eluded me long ago. I'm curious to learn more. Certain tastes must be acquired, and all things must happen in their own time. Well, this is another time and my tastes have evolved. I'd still have no appetite for an ersatz spiritual meal, but it might be safe now to put an authentic one back on my menu.

Lemon Cayenne Drink

For whatever bizarre reason, the moment I got home from India I went on a ten-day fast, something I'd never done before and haven't done since. All I consumed the entire time was this cleansing drink (you can have as many as you want in a day) and otherwise just water. Though I never felt hunger, I did have an overwhelming impulse to cook, so my family was served elaborate meals every night, while I stayed in the kitchen sipping my pious lemonade. Whatever weight I might have lost, they surely gained. Anyway, I still drink this sometimes, though more for just a morning or when I'm feeling under the weather, not for days on end.

MAKES 1 DRINK

2 tablespoons lemon juice
2 tablespoons maple syrup
¼ teaspoon cayenne pepper
1 cup/250 ml warm water

Mix together the lemon juice, maple syrup, and cayenne pepper, then stir in the water. Sip slowly.

Chicken Liver Pâté

If you're looking for a quick way to satisfy a craving for France, whip up this delectable pâté, toast some thinly sliced baguette, and pour yourself a glass of Burgundy.

MAKES ABOUT 1½ CUPS/375 ML (THREE ½-CUP/125-ML RAMEKINS)

1 cup/225 g unsalted butter, very soft, divided

1 medium-small onion, minced

1 teaspoon chopped fresh thyme leaves

1 bay leaf

¼ teaspoon allspice

1 teaspoon salt

⅛ teaspoon white pepper

1 pound/450 g chicken livers

1 garlic clove, grated

¼ cup/60 ml Cognac, Madeira, or whisky

Melt ¼ cup/60 g of the butter in a sauté pan. Add the onion, thyme, bay leaf, allspice, salt, and pepper, and cook gently until the onion is very soft, about 8 minutes. Turn up the heat, add the chicken livers, and cook until the outsides have coloured but the insides are still slightly pink, about 5 minutes. Add the garlic for a minute, then stir in the Cognac and remove from the heat.

Remove the bay leaf, and let the mixture cool to room temperature. (This is important, otherwise the hot mixture will melt the butter.) Purée in a food processor, then pulse in the remaining butter a pinch at a time until incorporated. Press through a sieve. Pack into three ½-cup/125-ml ramekins, wrap, and refrigerate, preferably for a day or two so the flavours can mellow. Remove from the fridge about 20 minutes before serving to bring to a spreadable consistency.

10

Initiations

Though it wasn't until my late twenties that I'd get a full immersion in French food, I did get a foreshadowing of the education to come a number of years earlier when I spent a month in Paris staying with a family friend. It started with morning coffee on the first day. My host, Andy, in his cerulean blue kitchen overlooking the boisterous rue d'Orsel, went about his brewing with the meticulousness of an alchemist. Like other Parisians I'd meet in years to come, rather than using a French press, he favoured an Italian stovetop espresso pot, the kind that screws apart in the middle. He filled the bottom with water, popped in the metal filter filled with coffee grounds, then screwed on the top and set it on a gas burner, which he lit with a match. As it was left to heat, the lid remained open, so you could watch as the coffee sputtered up through the central spout and pooled piping hot into the top of the pot. Meanwhile, on another burner, milk was warming, and when the steam rose, he whisked it briskly to a soft froth. This was back in the day when you could still drink your café crème (or what English speakers refer to as café au lait) from vintage bowls without it looking contrived, and that's what we'd do, dipping in rusks of bread between sips and peering out the window onto the street below, where fabric shops spilled into the street and women compared bolts of toile de Jouy and bold African cottons. Of course, coffee is not exactly fine dining, but the attention paid even to that little ritual was a signal to me that there were different expectations when it came to how food should be prepared and consumed in France.

One Sunday, Andy took me outside the city on the RER train to have lunch with friends somewhere along a canal. What would my idea of lunch have been at the time? I wonder. I was fresh out of university, just emerging from a stage of life when veggie-pâté sandwiches on whole grain bread had featured regularly, along with my favourite pasta invention: tin of mushroom soup, tin of tuna, chopped fresh dill, spaghetti (my mother would have had a fit). I thought that was gourmet.

We arrived at noon to find a table set up on the lawn covered in a cloth, adorned with flowers, and surrounded by chairs for about eight. I can't remember who was there. I didn't know anyone apart from Andy, and the only other vague memory is of the hostess, who seemed to have boundless energy and certainly a knack for dealing with boundless appetites. Let me make up a menu, because it's too far back for me to be accurate. We would have started with Champagne and gougères, those ubiquitous cheesy choux-pastry bites, along with some tiny pink radishes accompanied with butter and salt. After that, a basket of bread would have landed, possibly with Chablis splashed into our glasses, and a terrine of jambon persillé surrounded with cornichons. Next, a quiche, roughly the size of a stop sign, filled with ratatouille and chèvre and decorated with a baked-in zucchini flower spread-eagle on top. More white wine was surely served, or maybe rosé . . . whatever it was, there was a lot of it. Next a salade verte, to cleanse the palate, along with a platter of five different cheeses and a bottle of light red. At last, the final blow: an almond cake with marinated strawberries, followed by a deadly round of Mirabelle liqueur.

I was in my early twenties, active and hungry by definition, but that lunch truly did make me wonder if I wasn't going to explode. On it went, as the sun arced its narrative across the sky, ending at about five o'clock in the afternoon. We dropped our napkins on the table and went off in various directions to pass out on the grass for a siesta. A couple of hours later, I came to and gave a good look around trying to remember where I was. Ah yes. Lunch. The countryside. France. Parmi les fous.

Andy was nowhere to be seen, but someone mumbled he'd gone down to the canal for a stroll, so I scrambled off in search of him. I found him squatting with a camera pressed to his face, zooming in on a weeping willow at the water's edge. "I'm ready to go whenever you are," I said. "Go?" Andy said. "It's nearly time for aperitifs!" These people truly were crazy. Indeed, by the time we got back up to the house, our hosts were firing up the barbecue to grill chicken and merguez sausages, but first, a kir or two with some tapenade tartines. I'd never seen people eat so much in my life.

Andy was a photographer, busy every day setting up shoots for things like lipstick and skin toner, or rushing off to photography labs somewhere down around the Bastille. So, between meals, I left him alone and went exploring on my own. I have very few memories of that stay in general, but one is most certainly of the day I stumbled upon Dehillerin, the old-style kitchenware shop near les Halles. It has gone slightly downhill in recent years, in my opinion, but back then it was a dream. They had everything a kitchen could ever want, all of the highest quality, and gloriously displayed: copper pots, steel knives, balloon whisks the size of your head, every imaginable mould for cakes and chocolates you could conceive of.

I walked though Dehillerin like Alice in Wonderland, dazed and amazed. Though the shop was famous, I'd never heard of its existence and so felt I had discovered it. I think I felt I was the one and only person ever to discover Paris, too. It reminds me of Peter's son, Ben, reporting in from his first trip to Spain. "Dad!" he shouted excitedly down the telephone. "You're never going to believe it!" Peter bolted into an upright position on the sofa to take in the astonishing announcement to come. "You order a drink here," Ben continued, "and . . . THEY GIVE YOU FREE FOOD!" Ah to be young again, discovering Dehillerin and the five-hour lunch, like Ben discovering tapas, the whole wide world a banquet of possibilities.

Corn Tostadas with Avocado, Feta, and Pickled Red Onion

This recipe is not Spanish, obviously, but I like how the tostadas themselves almost serve as tapas plates. If you can't find tostadas, make your own by frying small corn tortillas, or do a soft version using flour tortillas. Yet another option is to serve this unassembled and in larger quantities as a casual first course. Simply arrange a block of feta, a few sliced avocados, a pile of fresh coriander leaves, a bowl of pickled red onion, and a spilling of lime wedges on a serving board. Pile tostadas on a plate alongside, and let people make their own.

For pickled red onion, thinly slice a red onion. Put ¾ cup/175 ml red wine vinegar in a saucepan along with 3 tablespoons sugar, ¼ teaspoon salt, a pinch of chili pepper flakes, and a bay leaf. Bring to a boil, add the onion, turn the heat down to low for half a minute, then remove from the heat and cool completely. This will fill a ½-pint mason jar. Store it in the fridge.

SERVES 4 AS AN APPETIZER

4 corn tostadas

1 perfectly ripe avocado

1½ ounces/45 g feta cheese, crumbled

4 forkfuls of pickled red onion or shallot

A handful each of fresh coriander leaves and torn mint leaves

Fleur de sel and freshly ground pepper

4 nicely trimmed lime wedges

Lay the tostadas on a serving board. Slice the avocado and divide amongst the tostadas. Scatter over the feta and pickled onion, followed by the coriander and mint leaves. Sprinkle on salt and grind over pepper. Arrange the lime wedges on the board to squeeze over the tostadas before eating.

Spinach Terrine with Parmesan Cream

You'll love the intense, smooth spinachiness of this French country terrine, and how the hint of Pernod lends it mystery. A nice way to get your greens without actually eating a mound of raw leaves. Serve as a starter.

FOR THE TERRINE

11 ounces/300 g spinach

2 tablespoons butter

1 tablespoon flour or cornstarch

1 cup/250 ml milk

3 ounces/90 g Gruyère, Comté, or white cheddar (about 1¼ cups, grated)

¾ teaspoon salt

Freshly ground pepper

A few grindings of freshly grated nutmeg, to taste

2 eggs plus 4 yolks

1 tablespoon Pernod

FOR THE SAUCE

1 cup/250 ml heavy cream

¾ cup/30 g finely grated Parmesan cheese

Salt and pepper

To make the terrine, butter a 4-cup/1-litre terrine mould and line the base with parchment. Heat the oven to 400°F/200°C.

Bring a large pot of water to a boil, salt it, and blanch the spinach for 4 minutes. Drain, rinse in ice-cold water, drain again, then squeeze into a tight ball with your hands held over the sink to get all the water out. Set aside.

Melt the butter in a small saucepan. When it foams, whisk in the flour, and cook for 1 minute to remove the raw flour taste. Whisk in the milk, and bring to a boil to thicken, stirring constantly. Remove from the heat, stir in the cheese to melt, and season with the salt, pepper, and nutmeg.

Purée the spinach and white sauce in a food processor until smooth, add the eggs and yolks and the Pernod, and pulse to blend completely. Pour the mixture into the prepared terrine mould, and bake until a knife inserted into the middle comes out clean, about 40 minutes. Remove from the oven and let sit for 10 to 15 minutes before unmoulding onto a platter or cutting board. (It can also be made ahead and served at room temperature.)

To make the sauce, put the cream and Parmesan into a saucepan and bring to a boil. Reduce by half. Taste, and season with salt and pepper. Slice the terrine, and serve warm with the sauce spooned around.

11

An Education

Le Chef

Occasionally, I receive letters from youngish people asking me if they should quit their jobs and run off to cooking school. It's a hard question to answer, because what I want to advise is "run for the hills!" But that might sound a bit suspect, since quitting a job and going off to cooking school is exactly what I once did myself. I'm not sure what possessed me, considering that I never had any ambition to cook in a professional kitchen, and besides I was already a fairly competent cook by the time I went, having been brought up in a household where every bite was produced from scratch. I suppose I must have imagined that home cooking wasn't the real thing, and that to be really good in the kitchen, I would need to get in on the secrets of cuisine gastronomique. Surely it could do no harm anyway. As I told myself at the time, "The worst thing that can happen is that you'll give better dinner parties."

Off I went, then, to a (now defunct) cooking school in Vancouver, keen to acquire the skills to make anything I wanted and to emerge with the palate of a true connoisseur. How adorable that I imagined this could be achieved in under six months, and in Western Canada alone! I bought the required uniform—baggy black-and-white chequered trousers and a crisp white chef's jacket—along with a red toolbox full of the requisite kit: fishbone tweezers, turning knife, candy thermometer, pastry scraper, and so on. Then, I tripped off to join about thirty other keeners in a classroom kitchen every day.

The kitchen was arranged much like a lecture hall, with the instructor's station front and centre and the student stations spaced around it in a ring. Every day, we were given demonstrations of a few dishes, then we'd set about replicating them ourselves, and finally we'd place our results on a main table so they could be compared, tasted, and evaluated. I remember being struck at the time by how every dish on the table always looked and tasted completely different, even though we'd all seen the same demonstration and followed exactly the same recipe. There's proof for you that each of us is inevitably an ingredient in every dish we make.

Anyway, all that was fine, though I can't say I loved the environment, which in addition to being rather industrial could also be competitive, high-pressure, and mean. I remember once getting so frustrated during the making of a croquembouche that I burst into tears (This is the end of the world!). And oh how I hated the "black box" exams, which involved creating a dish from a crate of mystery ingredients within a set period of time (tick tock, tick tock). The curriculum, too, was somewhat confusing, because it was trying to be an all-encompassing overview of virtually every cuisine on earth. One day we'd make Portuguese kale and sausage soup, the next day an Asian duck stock, on another curried lamb, and so on, so that, in the end, we had the equivalent of a pile of jigsaw pieces, none of which was from the same puzzle.

The school taught restaurant-style cooking, of course, which at the time I didn't realize was a completely different beast from home cooking. I just thought it was meant to be superior, food you'd call gourmet, and so, trusting in that supposition, I was quick to embrace every idea put before me about what that should be. At cooking school, vegetables, unless you were the lowest form of pond life, had to be cooked al dente, which for some bizarre reason was interpreted to mean merely blanched. (All these years later, whenever I encounter an underdone potato or carrot in a restaurant, I think to myself, "Cooking school strikes again.") When we plated dishes—and you always plated every dish, individually—we were told they had to have "height," so lamb chops got propped up against their accompanying mooshy peas like so many banjos against a beanbag chair, or you might stack up a sliced tomato with a few basil leaves sticking out the sides like grassy terraces on a high-rise, then dribble a moat of olive oil around it, add a few artful drops of balsamic vinegar, and call it a salad. (More like a house of cards, is what I think today.) Because individual plating was so indisputably de rigueur, rather than make dishes, per se, the done thing was to create components—say, wilted spinach, seared scallops, beurre blanc—ingredients whose acquaintance would only be made once they hit the plate. And, of course, there were fancy tricks like squirt bottles of fruit purée to Pollock around lava cakes, and ring moulds for shaping pretentious beds of mashed potatoes or tuna tartare.

Well, take all that great wisdom away with you and try to throw a dinner party at home. I remember one of my first after graduating at which everyone sat at the table writhing in hunger while I, in a perspiring flap between courses, took to deep-frying threads of ginger to put on top of crab cakes, and shaping quenelles of ice cream to be held in place in the middle of their ice-rink-sized plates by mats of pistachio dust. With all due respect, after cooking school I had a lot to unlearn.

Cooking schools—or at least professional training of some sort—have their place. Restaurants, along with any number of institutions such as hospitals or schools, require people who understand the ins and outs of high-volume cooking, the stamina required to withstand the long and grueling hours of the industry, and, in some cases, the rigours of haute cuisine. Cooking schools give students a taste of that, but for budding home cooks like me, there were better ways to learn.

By a stroke of luck, within a year of finishing at culinary school, I found myself in France, working for cooking teacher and cookbook author Anne Willan. For many years, Anne ran a successful professional school in Paris, similar to the Cordon Bleu. But by the time I met her, École de Cuisine La Varenne had been turned into a summer school for amateur gourmets, offering weeklong programmes out of Anne's country house. I helped run those programmes, which featured cooking classes, tastings, excursions, and plenty of fine meals, then the rest of the year I was put on to assisting with cookbooks, which meant recipe testing and, more often for me, researching, writing, and editing. Of course, I was also a member of the household during this time, so I took part in everyday routines such as market shopping, preparing meals, setting the table, and, of course, dining. It was through those quotidian tasks—just by living—that I got my best and most useful education.

In Anne's world, the only things that ever got plated were first courses, such as artichokes with hollandaise or chèvre-stuffed tomatoes on a croûte. Otherwise, everything was served family style on platters, which were set on warming plates on a sideboard at the head of the dining room so people could help themselves. We made things like long-simmered beef daubes, potato gratins, and salades Niçoise that included green beans that were actually cooked. I remember being shocked during a cooking demonstration for one of the summer programs when a chef made a salad of potato, shallot, mussels, capers, herbs, and vinaigrette that was—gasp—completely flat. Of course, being in rural France, virtually everything we ate was French, too, so no dish ever stuck out like a sore thumb by being oddly foreign. Gradually, I began to get a sense of what elevated home cooking should be—and one thing it should definitely not be, which is an attempt to replicate restaurant cooking.

Speaking of which, at some point during that era, I did a month-long apprenticeship in a starred restaurant in the south of France, organized by Anne, who wanted all her protégées to have an understanding of what life in a professional kitchen was really like. There wasn't much sleeping involved, I certainly remember. Days began at the crack of dawn and, with the exception of a short break after the lunch service, were spent standing until you hit the sack after midnight with a thud. Jobs were highly repetitive. One day you'd be handed a giant box of parsley and have to spend hours delicately removing each leaf, one by one. Another day, you'd find yourself before a vat of cooked trotters, feeling your way through the fatty mass with your fingertips, like reading braille, trying to pick out every bone so that the meat could be turned into a terrine that wouldn't choke someone to death. Then along would come another box of parsley the size of a Mack truck. Before anyone spends a small fortune on cooking school, an apprenticeship is advisable. If I had ever entertained even the slightest flicker of a notion that restaurant life might be for me, that stage certainly snuffed it out. Others thrived in that environment. One fellow parsley-leaf plucker from those days went on to work under one of the top chefs in Paris, and later opened his own restaurant in Tel Aviv. He had never been to cooking school. His entire education came from working for the best who would have him, starting with the most menial jobs imaginable and working his way up.

After that stage, I went straight back to home cooking where I belonged, thank goodness for my sake and everyone else's. But that has been its own education, one where the only way to learn is by doing. It was never cooking school that was going to teach me crucial things like how to get the roast turkey, gravy, stuffing, mashed potatoes, carrots, and brussels sprouts all to the table—hot—at the same time, but rather decades of Christmases. And though I may have been given a glimpse of knife skills back then, it has been all the chopping, slicing, and dicing that comes with making dinner every night that has trained my hands to use a blade. In the end, for me, a home kitchen has proved better than any classroom. And the mouths I've fed no doubt have been my greatest teachers. Just a few things to take into consideration, should you ever decide to drop everything and run off to cooking school.

Burnt Beans

Here's a recipe to make any recent cooking-school graduate (or Californian) cringe, because there is defiantly no crunch here. Instead, these green beans are deliberately cooked to confit and they are absolutely addictive, a house staple of Anne Willan's, whose recipe this is, from the Château du Feÿ days. Note that you don't want to make this with tiny fresh haricots verts, but with regular green beans, or with frozen beans, in which case the blanching won't be necessary.

SERVES 4

Salt
2 pounds/1 kg green beans
¼ cup/60 g butter
Pepper

Bring a large pot of water to a boil, salt it, and add the beans. Cook the beans to al dente, about 8 minutes. Drain, rinse in ice-cold water, and drain again. Cool completely.

To finish, melt the butter in a wok or large frying pan, add the beans, and cook over very low heat, tossing occasionally, until the beans are slightly scorched and very limp indeed, about 20 minutes. Season with salt and pepper.

Lemon Risotto with Fresh Peas and Tarragon

This is the brightest-tasting risotto I've ever put in my mouth, and it's the liberal hand with lemon juice that does it (about 2 tablespoons—don't skimp!). Strictly speaking, it doesn't need the peas and tarragon, but they do add a considered cheffy touch.

SERVES 4

2 tablespoons olive oil

1 small onion, minced

Salt

1½ cups/330 g arborio rice

1 garlic clove, grated

½ cup/125 g dry white wine

4 to 5 cups/1 to 1.25 litres clam stock or seafood stock

½ cup/65 g freshly shelled peas, blanched

Zest and juice of 1 lemon, plus more to taste

¾ cup/30 g finely grated Parmesan cheese

2 to 3 tablespoons butter

A small handful of fresh tarragon and/or basil leaves, gently torn

Pepper

Heat the oil in a medium, heavy-bottomed saucepan. Add the onion and salt to taste, and gently fry on medium-low until soft, but not browning, 10 to 15 minutes. Increase the heat to medium, add the rice, and stir for a minute or two until a white dot appears in the centre of each grain. Add the garlic, then pour in the wine and stir until it evaporates, a matter of minutes. Meanwhile, bring the stock to a simmer in a pot.

Once the wine has vanished, add ½ cup of stock to the rice and keep it

Continued on the next page

at a simmer as you stir constantly until the rice has completely absorbed the liquid. Continue in the same manner, adding a ladleful of stock at a time, until the rice is tender and the whole mixture still soupy, 20 to 25 minutes in all. (If you run out of stock, you can continue with hot water.)

When the risotto has finished cooking, add the lemon zest and juice and the Parmesan. Taste and adjust the salt and lemon, as needed. Stir in the butter. To serve, ladle the risotto into warm soup plates, scatter the peas and herbs over the top, and garnish with freshly ground pepper.

12

Thank U

My late father-in-law was a great one for researching products before taking out his wallet. He'd study up on absolutely everything from restaurants to sound systems to shoes to safaris before he'd settle on what he was happy to pay for. A neighbour of mine has the same gene, which is why the taps on her new kitchen sink, scrutinized before purchase and analysed against virtually every other model on the market, are about as elaborate and sturdy as the wheelhouse on an ocean liner. Doing her homework was worth the effort, because she now has taps that will last her a lifetime and give her enormous joy every time she washes a muffin tin, rinses grapes, or soaks a pair of wool mittens. There's a lesson in all this about how to find bliss on a daily basis.

Inspired by those two sticklers for buying right the first time, I'm tempted to go through my kitchen and give every item the love test, tossing out anything that puts a frown on my face and replacing it with something smile-inducing. The citrus juicer, if its ears are burning, will be trying to hide behind the coffeemaker right now, because it's certainly near the top of my list of rejects. It's plastic and gets clogged with seeds and pith, making it a nightmare to clean. (What I want is one of those vintage metal numbers that looks something like a potato ricer. One size fits all citrus fruits and it empties the skins of their nectar neatly and completely.) There are a few ugly, flimsy plastic utensils that entered my life with Peter, and they poke out disturbingly amongst the wooden spoons in the kitchen-tool crock like dead stems in an otherwise vibrant bouquet. The hideous black ladle with stainless-steel handle, for instance, must go. And there's also that whisk with the handle so heavy that if you accidentally leave it in a pot of béchamel it will back-flip over the side and onto the floor, leaving a spray of thick white sauce in its wake. These may sound like small things, but they take a cumulative toll on one's ability to maintain a state of serenity, so if that's at all a goal then it's worth surrounding oneself with objects that help make life smooth, pleasant, and even delightful.

I recall someone once saying of my late grandfather, "Gordon won't buy small, but he'll buy big." It was a reference to the fact that he would spare no expense on large equipment, but when it came to, say, replacing an old can opener with a new one, it was like pulling teeth on an alligator. Thinking on it, I'm not sure that was such a unique trait. Many of us have a tendency to splash out on out-of-the-ordinary items (barbecues, televisions, and downhill skis must all be top of the line), but then skimp when it comes to ordinary things that get banal, everyday use, such as toothbrushes, coat hangers, vegetable peelers, and tea towels. And yet, how maddening it is when these everyday things fail us: the corkscrew so weak that its arms fall off just as you're trying to open springtime's first rosé, the good-for-nothing pepper grinder that yields no more than a speck of

Tellicherry dust a minute, the spatula so stiff it leaves half the cake batter behind on the sides of the bowl.

While I'm on about this, let me tell you my pepper-grinder story. It was just after cooking school when I was keen to acquire all the best kitchen equipment I could lay my hands on, and I was having lunch at a café cum kitchen-supply shop with a couple of friends. On our table was a handsome, shiny red pepper grinder which I picked up to use on my salad. Well! The grind was so perfect I'd never experienced anything like it, and the object so handsome, I had to have it. Seventy bucks, bought right off the table. Score!

But, as we were driving away from the place in friendly silence, jarringly, one of my friends suddenly blurted out, "Are you IN-SANE?" "What are you talking about?" I asked, completely mystified. And she bellowed, "Seventy dollars on a pepper grinder? A pepper grinder!?!?" (Keep in mind this was a good twenty-five years ago.) After another mile of road, tortured over the possibility that my purchase might indeed have been a folly, I turned back and returned the thing to the shop. To make a long story short, hundreds of dollars and several years' worth of maddening, dysfunctional pepper grinders later, I eventually ended up buying myself the model I'd originally wanted. It lives on my kitchen counter to this day.

Sometimes perfect function in a tool is enough to make it lovable, but it's even better when there's a charm factor involved. For example, I'm staying at a friend's heritage house right now and all the rooms have bricks for doorstoppers, only you'd never know they were bricks because each one is wrapped in gorgeous, thick, textured Japanese paper. Every single doorstop is a little bijou! My heart positively leapt the time I encountered black, beeswax-covered dental floss in a tiny metal salt-shaker-like container. Whoever thought of turning teeth flossing into a moment of enjoyment? I once spotted a beech table-crumb sweeper with silk bristles so beautiful that it immediately made me want to turn a bread basket upside down over the table and let the crumbs hail down so I could have the satisfaction of brushing them off with all the tender, loving care you'd put into grooming a prized stallion. The neighbour with the enviable kitchen sink I mentioned has, of all things, small golden handles attached to every toilet seat in the house so you never have to come in contact with the porcelain. I mean, come on! If you can turn even lifting a toilet seat into a little thrill, you're a genius.

The reason for all this ruminating about everyday objects is that I recently read about something called Ayudha Puja, a wonderful-sounding day at the end of the Hindu nine-nights festival, Navratri, which is dedicated to the worship of instruments. In olden times, apparently people bowed down to things like their ploughs and swords, acknowledging the vital role they played in their lives and the way these instruments connected them to the divine. If anyone today still observes the practice (and I'm told they do), perhaps they're more apt to worship things like their computers, lawn mowers, or rice cookers. Who knows? But what a lovely idea, it struck me, to consider stopping once a year to pay respect to the things that get us through our harried lives on a daily basis, all those faithful servants, those indispensable extensions of ourselves that too often we take for granted. So, sing it, Alanis! Thank you, India . . . Thank you, Cheese Grater . . . Thank you, Disinfectant . . . Thank you, Oven Mitt . . . Thank you, Pot Scraper . . . Thank you, thank you, Appliance!

Green Juice

Given how much I've groaned on about what real-estate hogs small appliances can be, it's a bit hypocritical to turn around and give you a recipe that requires a juicer. However, the body loves fresh juice so much that making it is bound to become a habit, and the machine will earn its keep. This recipe comes from my admirably fit and health-conscious neighbour who drinks this delicious elixir every day and swears by its benefits to well-being.

SERVES 2

2 celery ribs, trimmed

1 packed cup Tuscan kale leaves, about 1 ounce/30 g

½ Granny Smith apple, cored and cut into pieces

¼ bunch of flat-leaf parsley or coriander leaves

¼ bunch of fresh mint leaves

1-inch/2.5-cm piece of fresh ginger, peeled

1 to 2 limes, quartered

Salt

Feed the celery, kale, apple, parsley, mint, ginger, and limes into a juicer, and juice according to the manufacturer's instructions. Skim off any foam, then season with salt, if you like. Pour into glasses and consume immediately to get maximum nutritional value.

Beet Carpaccio with Herbs and Horseradish Cream

Thank you, mandoline slicer! That's the key to getting perfectly even, ultra-thin slices of beet, which turn the humble root vegetable into a salad that feels glamourous and grand. Serve as a first course for a dinner party or scale it up in size to add to a summer buffet.

SERVES 4

FOR THE BEETS

Salt

1 pound/450 g red or golden beets (about 2 medium)

10 anchovies, chopped

About 1 tablespoon pine nuts or chopped pistachios

Torn leaves from a mix of fresh herbs (parsley, coriander, dill, mint, basil, chives, etc.)

Olive oil, for drizzling

Lemon zest, removed with a zesting tool and chopped

Fleur de sel and freshly cracked pepper

FOR THE HORSERADISH CREAM

¼ cup/60 ml heavy cream

Salt and pepper

1 to 2 tablespoons horseradish, plus more to taste

To make the beets, bring a pot of water to a boil. Add salt and the beets and cook until just tender, anywhere from 30 to 45 minutes, depending on the size. Cool, peel, and trim, then slice very thin on a mandoline.

Arrange the slices in concentric circles on 4 serving plates. Scatter over the anchovies, pine nuts, and herbs, drizzle with olive oil, sprinkle with the lemon zest, and season with salt and pepper.

To make the horseradish cream, whip the cream, season with salt and pepper, then whip in the horseradish. Divide amongst the plates, putting a spoonful in the centre of each, and serve.

13

The Dishwashers

There was a dishwasher in my childhood house, briefly. I can vaguely picture its square bulk, squatted between the pantry and the back-stairs door, a second-hand machine passed on to us by an enthusiastic relative. My mother never had terribly high hopes for it, and indeed it never proved its worth. Amongst other things, it was soon blamed for balling up the septic tank, which at the time consisted of two molasses puncheons (oak casks) rigged up with pipes, still there from when the house first got "plumbing" in 1953.

As luck would have it, one day the dishwasher suddenly stopped working. My mother shipped it out the door with the neighbourhood handyman for repair, and he returned in a week, perplexed, and presented her with a pair of scissors. "These were wedged into the machinery somehow," he said. My brothers and I exchanged sheepish glances. "Thank you for the scissors," my mother said. "Keep the dishwasher." Thus, the vicissitudes of daily dishwashing by hand became a routine part of my life, and, over time, made me into an expert on the practice. I'm always pleased to enlighten less-fortunate souls (i.e., people who grew up with dishwashers) on all they've missed out on.

There are three stages to dishwashing, at least when three children are assigned the task: washing, drying, and putting away. My older brother, Gordon, and I came to almost nightly blows over the fact that he far too often declared himself "put-er awayer," which meant he didn't have to show up for duty until my little brother, Stephen, and I had almost finished the real work. "Put-er awayer" didn't even count as helping as far as I, chief washer, was concerned. Sometimes Gordon dried, but he only ever lasted halfway through because, if I was washing, we'd have got into a screaming match by then and my mother would have threatened us with "the pickle stick." (Leave it to our house to have one of those.) More often, Gordon threw in the towel and stormed off in a silent rage, leaving me up to my elbows in soapy water, incensed.

When I was thirteen or so, I had a home economics teacher called Mrs. Montgomery who, in addition to drilling into our heads that "ladies squat down with knees together to pick things up; they do not bend over from the waist," instructed the grade-seven girls of Rothesay Junior High School in the intricate science of washing up. I memorized every crucial detail: rinse and stack dirty dishes first; sink full of hot, soapy water on the left; sink of hot clear rinsing water on the right; begin with the glasses because they are the least dirty; soak cutlery (but not knives) at the bottom while doing the plates; always save pots and pans for last; change the water throughout, as necessary. Gordon always managed to wash a pot before he'd finish all the glasses. That drove me right out of my skull.

I got to be quite a tyrant at the sink, what with all that academic training on the subject of dishes. I'm afraid the tendency has never left me. When I worked at Anne Willan's cooking school in France in my twenties, I earned the title of "champion washer-upper." I was rather put out by that at the time (I was, after all, trying to become champion cook, not queen of the dish pit!) but, upon reflection, perhaps it wasn't so bad to be recognized as having some talent at making order out of chaos, which, I suppose, is what effective dish-washing is.

It's a wonder that large corporations, instead of spending fortunes on organizational psychologists to put their CEOs through obstacle courses at ski resorts as a work-style test, don't simply set them all up washing dishes together for an afternoon. The "washer" has to do all the dishes in the right order and not forget to rinse; the "dryer" has to move fast enough and be thorough; the "put-er awayer" has to show up on time so that dry dishes don't start crashing over the end of the clean, dry dishes spot on the counter. How my brothers and I weaseled out of roles, attempted short-cuts, and argued over every minute detail, over and over again, night after night! Oh, it's all revealing, believe me. As my father used to say, "Your mother and I have only had one fight in our entire marriage . . . and we've had it about three thousand times."

My father had his own special way of dealing with dishes. He cooked a lot and still does, especially when the weather is bad and he can't spend the whole live-long day in his garden. At six A.M. he'll already be downstairs banging around with pans and spoons and timers, and by the time everyone else emerges, the counter will be stacked with cookies and cakes; there will be a casserole in the oven, bread rising under a tea towel, pancakes frying . . . and every blessed pot, dish, cup, saucepan, strainer, bowl, and whisk in the house will have been hurled into the sink, like landfill, for the dishes fairy to contend with.

There were occasions, however, when he appeared to love doing dishes, like during those endless extended-family dinners we hosted every holiday. My father ate faster than the rest of us, and the split second the last fork had been laid down, he was on his feet, tearing away the plates from under everyone's noses and darting out to the kitchen to start scrubbing. Sometimes, he'd miss a whole course because he was out there slaving away at the sink while we ate. Poor Dad, I used to think. Now I realize: hmm . . .

I always figured it would come up one day. I'd be planning my life (and my kitchen) with some unsuspecting man of my dreams and, with all the best intentions, he'd try to steer me into an appliance shop. There and then, we'd have the first major row of our relationship. But, in fact, it has never happened. Peter doesn't mind doing dishes by hand with me, and in fact he even appreciates it as a peaceful way to reconnect after a busy dinner. That's at least one argument we don't have to worry about having three thousand times.

One-Pan Chocolate Cake

This recipe, taught to me by my "aunt," Nancy, when I was little, can, in fact, truly be a one-pan cake, mixed in the very dish you bake it in. I confess that when I make it now I prefer to whisk everything in a bowl and pour it into a tin lined with parchment. Whichever way you do it, the result will be a handsome, family-friendly cake, attractively topped with a rubble of melted chocolate chips and buttery pecans.

MAKES ONE 8-INCH/20-CM CAKE

½ cup/125 ml vegetable oil

2 ounces/60 g unsweetened chocolate

¾ cup/175 ml water

1 cup/200 g sugar

1 egg

1¼ cups/155 g flour

½ teaspoon salt

½ teaspoon baking soda

1 teaspoon vanilla

6 ounces/170 g semisweet chocolate chips

⅓ cup/40 g pecans, chopped

Heat the oven to 350°F/180°C. Put the oil and unsweetened chocolate in an 8-inch/20-cm cake pan and place it in the oven until the chocolate melts, about 4 minutes. Remove from the oven and add the water, sugar, egg, flour, salt, baking soda, and vanilla. Mix smooth with a fork and spread evenly over the pan. Now, sprinkle over the chocolate chips and nuts. Bake until a toothpick inserted in the centre comes out clean, about 40 minutes. Cool, cut, and serve.

Fish en Papillote

Fish and a green vegetable, with a smattering of Asian flavours, make a full meal in a paper packet, perfect when you're craving something light, though some might like a small bowl of steamed rice on the side or perhaps a buckwheat noodle salad to add some heft to the menu. As is, the washing up afterwards is virtually nil.

SERVES 2

Salt

1 large bok choy, quartered if very large

2 fillets of cod, halibut, sea bass, or other firm, white fish (about 10 ounces/280 g in all)

Pepper

1 green onion, sliced

1 garlic clove, sliced

½-inch/1.25-cm piece of fresh ginger, peeled and sliced into fine julienne

½ small Thai red chili pepper, seeded and minced

2 teaspoons soy sauce

2 teaspoons fish sauce

A drizzle of sesame oil

2 lime wedges, for serving

Heat the oven to 350°F/180°C.

Bring a pot of water to a boil, salt it, and add the bok choy. Cook for 3 to 4 minutes, then drain, rinse in cold water, and drain again. Pat dry with a clean tea towel.

Cut two relatively large pieces of parchment. Lay half the vegetable in the middle of each for a base. Lay the fish on top, and season lightly with salt

Continued on the next page

and pepper. Scatter the green onion, garlic, ginger, and chili over each, then dribble over the soy sauce, fish sauce, and sesame oil. Seal the packages and set on a baking sheet.

Bake until the fish is just cooked (130°F/54°C), about 20 minutes. Set the packages on serving plates with lime wedges within reach, slash open the tops with scissors or a sharp knife, and eat.

14

Toast

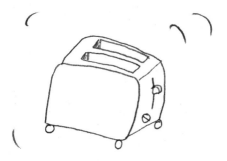

"What is it with you Brits and your little metal toast stands?" I was asking my friend Bill. "Oh, they're essential," he told me. "All they seem to do is make the toast cold," I argued, and he cried back, "That's the whole point!"

It is?

We were talking about toast made from thin white bread of the commercial variety. Bill explained that once it's toasted, it should be wrapped in a towel so that as it cools it retains its moisture, then it goes into the toast stand with an apparently desirable cold, thin, slightly leathery chewiness, which is the preferred toast texture for people who like their butter not to melt. He also opined that Marmite is better on cold toast. At any rate, this is how his mother ate her toast every day of the week (and you can't argue with Mum), except on Sundays, when she had it hot, presumably without any toast-stand intervention, and with butter all a-dribble beneath the marmalade.

Even the least gastronomic amongst us considers himself a connoisseur of some thing or other, namely those that we have consumed so many times we feel a certain ownership about them. Toast, for most of us, is one such food. Personally, I would have thought one of the first qualities a connoisseur would expect of toast is that it be hot, but to each his own. Peter tells a nice story of his school days when the refectory had one of those toast rotisserie devices that you sometimes see in hotel breakfast rooms. Every day a different boy from each table would be assigned the job of toast fetcher, which meant they had to line up, pick up bread for the table, insert it into that Ferris wheel for Wonder bread, and wait for it to tumble back out golden brown. The last piece to come out was obviously the warmest slice, and the toast fetcher always had the special privilege of getting that piece for himself.

My own early memories of toast are of sick days home from school in bed. My mother was absolutely genius about taking care of us when we were in that condition. We'd get cold compresses for our foreheads, foot rubs, endless reading material, and regular deliveries of toast—not just any toast, I hasten to add, but toast with butter and red currant jelly, very importantly cut into triangles. It was only when we were sick that we got triangle toast, and I swear it could cure anything.

This reminds me of another toast memory from childhood, which is that we owned (and God only knows it's still in the house) some sort of metal bread-grilling device from days of old that was used over hot coals (you see similar mechanisms for holding whole fish over a campfire). It was brought out occasionally on weekends and always made toast a bit of an adventure. When the coals in the wood-stove were just right, we'd lay a couple of slices of brown bread into the contraption, close it, slide the metal ring up the handle to hold the two sides together, then hover it over the heat until the bread crispened and blistered. Fire adds a whole new dimension to toast that electricity can never replicate.

The French also have "toast" (or pain grillé), except for when there's something on top of it, in which case it becomes a "tartine." It's a very different experience from English toast from a metal toast stand. I remember one café in Paris that served a breakfast of ficelle (a sort of mini baguette) halved lengthwise and arranged in a napkin-lined basket, delivered warm ("warm as toast" had to come from somewhere!), along with a little pot of butter and some apricot jam to "tartiner" on top. That, with a steaming cup of milky coffee, might just be the single most wonderful solo-dining experience known to man, best had at a café table outside in a neighbourhood with choice people-watching potential.

The "tartine" concept is one that gets trotted out at the aperitif hour, too, although at that time of day it's a different beast. If it's baguette, it gets sliced into small rounds, rather than into logs that are halved. And, of course, this is not the time for Nutella or confiture, but rather for savoury toppings, such as tapenade or crushed fava beans with fresh chèvre and a drizzle of oil, or maybe some duck liver pâté or rillettes de porc. In this incarnation, it's the French equivalent of the Italian "crostini," and a saviour for people like me who are quite hopeless at coming up with little bites to serve with drinks. Spanish tapas go beyond toast, obviously, but it's nonetheless critical to that buffet spread as well, the most famous probably being pan con tomate. I remember the first time I was introduced to that: a toasted slice of bread from a boule, swiped first with a split clove of garlic, then rubbed with the cut side of a tomato, which the rough surface of the toast grates into a layer of cool, fruity purée, and finally drizzled with olive oil and sprinkled with salt. Once again, that and a glass of cold wine on a terrace looking out onto the world is a solitary moment of heaven.

There is no toaster in this house at present, though we do have one in storage that this trip down toast lane is making me want to dig out again. It's one of those frightfully expensive hand-built English models, a Dualit, which goes so far as to include the name of the assembler on the base plate of each toaster and which, rather than popping automatically, has a lever you lift up and down to monitor the toast's progress. It has slots wide enough to accommodate things like thick sourdough toast, bagels, and crumpets, not just thin white bread on its way to a metal toast stand. Taking into account the attention to detail in that toaster's design, you have to give it to the English for turning the crispening of a humble slice of bread into the stuff worthy of an academic paper.

And that reminds me of an incident several years ago at a private club in London. I had a breakfast meeting with two posh guys who I immediately sniffed out as coming from closed circles of the Mitford-esque variety. You know the types I mean: they know one set of rules for living, theirs, and if you do one thing wrong, such as say "nice to meet you," or put your milk in first (which, incidentally, I've never done), you're written off immediately. I thought to myself, "I'd better keep this simple," so I ordered toast and tea. Well, dumb. Arrives a metal stand containing a parade of cold, white toast and I suddenly had no idea what to do with it. At the time, I'd spent so long in France that English ways of doing things had grown fuzzy. In France, it's hands above the table; in England hands below, I remembered that. "It's toast, you idiot," said a voice in my head. In France, I would have torn off a piece of bread at a time to butter and eat, but for some reason it seemed like the wrong way to go with slices of Tesco Toastie, or whatever it was. And so, it sat there untouched, while I sipped my tea, starving. Only about five minutes before the meeting ended, the light went on. Oh right, butter a corner, bite that, then butter the next bite . . . The French way would have been perfectly acceptable, too, it turns out, but by then, it was too late anyway. The looks on their faces told me what I already knew: what was toast was moi.

Kimchi Tuna Melts

Toast, of course, can be turned into a meal unto itself, as with these hot, open-faced lunchtime delights. If you've never tasted the match made in heaven that is cheddar cheese and kimchi (Korea's famous fermented cabbage), you must make them without delay. We keep a jar of kimchi from the grocer in the fridge at all times just for these. If you're not up for the tuna melt, do at least venture into the land of kimchi grilled cheese. I'll leave you to improvise.

SERVES 2 OR 3

Drain a tin of tuna and tip it into a bowl. Break it up with a fork, and add ½ teaspoon Dijon mustard, 3 tablespoons mayonnaise, 2 tablespoons minced celery, 2 tablespoons sliced green onion, and a few grinds of the peppermill. Lightly toast 3 slices of white bread in a toaster oven, and remove.

Spread the tuna mixture evenly over the toasts, top with a generous layer of kimchi (about ¼ cup/40 g per toast), then top each with about ⅓ cup/30 g grated aged orange cheddar cheese to cover.

Pop them back in the toaster oven and broil for a minute or two until the cheese is melted and bubbling, keeping an eye on it because it goes fast. Remove to plates and garnish, if you like, with a few shards of green onion cut on the diagonal or fresh coriander leaves.

Red Currant Jelly

This indispensable jelly is delicious not only on toast, but also served with cheese or alongside terrines, pâtés, roasted meats, and of course in chicken sandwiches. I have been known to add a spoonful or two of it to wine sauce for things like duck as well. A most useful and versatile preserve.

MAKES FOUR 8-OUNCE/225-G JARS

2.2 pounds/1 kg red currants with stems (which are necessary for
  their pectin content)
About 1 cup/250 ml water, plus more if needed
Sugar

Pick over the currants, removing any leaves but keeping the berries on their stems, and put them in a large pot. Crush with a potato masher, and add enough water to cover the bottom of the pan and prevent the berries from burning. Cover, and bring to a simmer until the juices flow, about 5 minutes. Run through a coarse sieve.

Line a strainer with clean muslin or place a fine sieve within a larger one over a pot or bowl. Put the berries in, cover, and leave overnight to strain through. Next day, press the berries gently to extract as much juice as possible (some say not to do this to avoid clouding the jelly, but really it doesn't get that cloudy and, besides, why waste the juice?).

Measure the juice into a pot, cup by cup, and for every cup of juice add ¾ cup/150 g sugar. Bring the mixture to a boil and simmer until it reaches the jelling point. You can test by putting a spoonful on a plate that you've kept in the freezer. When pushed with a finger, the jelly should wrinkle. (If you prefer to use a thermometer, the jelly is done when it reaches 220°F/105°C.)

Pour the jelly, hot, into sterilized jars and screw the lids on tightly. As they cool, the tops will seal. Label the jars and store in a cool, dark place.

15

Very Grounding

Many years ago, I was seated beside my father at a big family meal and the dish before us, whatever it was, contained large pieces of beef. I must have been spending rather a long time wrestling with mine because my father eventually snapped: "Are you going to eat that or operate on it?" I returned a fuming hard stare and spoke in my defense: "I don't. Like. The grussle [*sic*]!"

You never see meat with gristle in it these days, but back then, perhaps because it would have been local beef, not necessarily butchered by anyone who really knew what they were doing, it regularly came thickly veined with inedible cartilage that was difficult enough even for adults to work their way around, never mind a preschooler. If it hadn't been in the days when children were expected to eat whatever they were served and to clear their plates, I'd have given it a pass and demanded, like today's fledgling humans, a plate of buttered carbohydrates in its stead. No luck. When I was growing up, children did not call the shots, so I had to carry on beavering my way through it.

To this day, I'm a cheap date in a steakhouse, and I do marvel at the way some men, in particular, get seriously excited about the prospect of a Bistecca alla Fiorentina or an ultra-thick Côte de Boeuf. At home, I haven't cooked meat in ages because it's Peter who likes to fire up the grill and mess around with ribs all afternoon, and it is he who hovers over the steak au poivre or lamb chops on a cast-iron-pan kind of night. More recently, he has taken over stews as well, which leaves me very much in a side-dish position in our kitchen, with one exception: ground meats.

At first glance, a heap of minced flesh isn't the sort of thing that immediately summons the Muses, but over these past several years of having packets of it plunked on the kitchen counter for me to deal with, I have come to appreciate its virtues, which are not, contrary to popular belief, restricted to the fact that a little goes a long way and that it's relatively cheap. It's the versatility of ground meat that turns out to be the real marvel, but I'll get to that in a minute.

First, we must discuss that thing called a "burger," almost always prefixed by the word "great." Why always "great burger," when it's just a burger? I grip my head in my hands whenever I hear the refrain because, let's face it, ground beef in a split bun is pretty banal. And it only gets worse when people try to chic it up by doing things like using rich and unyielding brioche buns, or topping an overly thick, all-dressed patty of meat with seared foie gras. But whether a burger of the gourmet or fast-food breed, the real problem I see with the invention is the stacking issue. There was a highly popular cookbook series a number of years ago which sparked a tsunami of sales in white plates, a widespread trend in ultra-minimalist photography, and a penchant for piling ingredients one on top of another like some kind of edible cheer-leading squad, and declaring the result a dish. Nothing wrong with that per se, except that it does mean there's no fusion, no melding, no chance for the whole to become more than the sum of its parts, which is what cooking is largely about. This is one reason why I have never liked burgers. They're a stacking job. No alchemy.

Until . . . ah, well! I have friends who, for years, have been trying to get me to believe that on the vast open plains of bad "great burgers," there does roam an actual great, and they finally invited me to try one. I will be scoffed at for being the last to arrive at the "smashburger" party, popularized by the New York chain Shake Shack. Gone the dense, tough puck of meat, murdered in ketchup and tucked between two hard mattresses. Instead, what you get is a soft potato bun that squishes down to its thin toasted underside so that it just mats the beef patty, which is skinny and crisp-edged, yet nonetheless full of squelching juicy fat. What goes on top doesn't matter (there's a "special sauce" and I think a crisp leaf of lettuce on the classic); it's the fact that, by this design, the layers meld, allowing the burger, at last, to become more than the sum of its parts.

This burger discovery happened toward the tail end of what I would call my "Ground Meat Grand Tour." I'd turned my back on ground meat for a long time, because I was bored and uninspired by hum-drum dishes from my own culinary heritage, such as spaghetti and meatballs or cottage pie. Then, gradually, I started to notice dishes from other countries involving ground meat, and they had some serious appeal. Thai larb, for example, captured my imagination: that delicious salad of ground pork (or beef, lamb, or chicken), spiced with hot chili, salted with fish sauce, and loaded with cooling herbs. You can spoon it onto lettuce boats and eat it with your hands, or you can serve it with shards of white cabbage, slices of cucumber, and lime wedges (very refreshing, which is not a word I'd normally associate with ground meat). Then I ventured into the terrain of kofta from the Middle East, lamb this time, warmly spiced with cumin, coriander, and fennel seed, packed into ovals on skewers, flavoured with a bit of char from the grill, and served with yoghurt sauce and flatbread. Romanian mititei, a street food, completely blew my mind when a friend made them for me, those exquisitely textured garlicky sausages scented with paprika and thyme that produce their own "skin" thanks to a mystery ingredient that turns out to be baking soda. Another friend steered me in the direction of Swedish meatballs, bathing in a creamy, beef-broth sauce with nary a bottle of ketchup in sight. A bit retro, but still . . . I did not grow up in a world where "ground meat" and "exotic" ever made it into the same sentence. Suddenly this had changed.

Socially, if asked what "cut" we'd like to be perceived as, we'd probably all insist on being a crown roast, but can you see, as I have, how boring that's starting to look? A crown roast can only ever be a crown roast. But ground meat, that maverick, that chameleon, can be whatever it likes, whenever it wants: Bolognese today, stuffed eggplant tomorrow, taco filling next week . . . It's a freedom fighter, a genuine artiste.

A million years ago, I clipped a recipe for meatloaf from out of *Vogue* (*Vogue*, of all places!). It was apparently one of fashion designer Bill Blass's favourite entertaining dishes. Americans like to do that once they're very rich or powerful, or both: display down-to-earthedness via food, such as by rolling up their sleeves and getting photographed eating a hotdog or burger (every president ever). Bill Blass apparently did it with meatloaf at his dinner parties. Well, one night, after a year or more of not going near a single North American approach to ground meat, I found myself craving something plain and comforting, and I thought, "If Bill Blass could do it . . . well?" So, I made meatloaf, even topped it with one of those questionable glazes involving ketchup, and wouldn't you know we devoured the whole thing. What can I say? Sometimes we crave exotic trips, but eventually we're thrilled to get home.

Thai Meat Salad with Sticky Rice and Garnishes (Larb)

A friend sent me this recipe once with the note, "You need this in your life," and as soon as I tried it I knew she was right! The list of ingredients appears long, but it's simple and quick to assemble. A light supper for warm nights, and fun to eat, too: just spoon the meat salad into lettuce boats, garnish, and lift them to your lips with your hands.

SERVES 4

FOR THE DRESSING

1 tablespoon Thai sticky rice (optional)

3 to 4 tablespoons fish sauce

2 teaspoons sugar

2 tablespoons lime juice

¼ teaspoon Thai chili powder, plus more to taste

FOR THE RICE

2 cups/500 g Thai sticky rice

2½ cups/625 ml water

1½ teaspoons salt

FOR THE MEAT SALAD

1 tablespoon oil

1 pound/450 g ground beef, pork, or chicken

4 garlic cloves, minced

1 large shallot, thinly sliced

2 Thai red chili peppers, thinly sliced

Continued on the next page

Large handfuls of fresh coriander, mint, and Thai basil (not
    chopped), plus more for garnish
A drizzling of sesame oil

FOR THE GARNISH
Bibb lettuce leaves or romaine hearts
Sliced cucumber
Lime wedges
⅓ cup/40 g roasted, salted peanuts, roughly chopped

For the dressing, first fry the tablespoon of rice, if using, in a dry frying pan until toasted and light brown. Grind in a clean coffee grinder, then whisk together in a small bowl with the fish sauce, sugar, lime juice, and chili powder and set aside.

For the rice, rinse the grains well in a colander under cold water, drain well, then put in a saucepan with the water and salt. Bring to a boil, covered, then reduce to a simmer and cook until the rice has absorbed all the water, 5 to 7 minutes. Turn off the heat, remove the lid, lay a clean tea towel over the rice, and replace the lid. Leave until serving so that the towel absorbs any excess moisture.

For the meat salad, heat the oil in a frying pan, add the meat, and cook until done, 5 to 7 minutes, adding the garlic during the last minute. Tip the meat into a bowl, add the shallot, chili peppers, herbs, and dressing, then toss thoroughly, transfer to a serving dish, and drizzle with a little sesame oil.

Arrange the lettuce leaves, cucumber slices, and lime wedges on a platter, along with the peanuts in a small bowl. Using another small bowl as a mould, pack it full of rice, then turn it out onto a platter. Continue with the rest of the rice making mounds, then garnish with some extra coriander and mint leaves. Serve with the meat salad.

Romanian Sausages

According to a Romanian friend, these "mititei" or "mici" (pronounced "meech") are the most popular summer food in her country. Normally, they're made with ground beef and/or pork, but she herself makes a chicken version which tastes like the best wings you've ever had, with a mysterious, golden "skin" forming on the outside when they grill. Follow the instructions exactly (they are unusual), and the results will be delectable. (Note the sausages must be prepared a day before they're cooked; and that they require beef stock that contains its natural gelatine.) Serve with ballpark mustard and beer.

MAKES 12

1 pound/450 g ground pork, beef, turkey, or chicken

4 garlic cloves, grated

1 teaspoon salt

A generous grinding of black pepper

½ teaspoon paprika

¼ teaspoon ground coriander

⅛ teaspoon ground allspice

½ teaspoon baking soda, dissolved in a tablespoon of sparkling water

1 teaspoon chopped fresh thyme leaves

⅓ cup/75 ml beef stock, cold

Olive oil, for shaping

A day before you plan to serve the sausages, put the meat, garlic, salt, pepper, paprika, coriander, allspice, baking soda mixture, thyme, and stock into the bowl of a stand mixer with the paddle attachment and mix for a full 10 minutes, during which time the texture of the meat will become a smooth, almost dough-like paste.

Continued on the next page

Coat your hands with olive oil and shape cylinders roughly 3 inches/ 3.5 cm long and 1 inch/2.5 cm in diameter, setting them in a lined container as you go. Alternatively, you can put the meat mixture into a plastic bag, cut off a tip, and pipe out the sausages. Cover and refrigerate overnight. Uncover the next day and leave refrigerated that way for a few hours to dry out somewhat. Remove from the fridge, still uncovered, for an hour before grilling.

Grill on the barbecue over high heat, turning occasionally and allowing them to take on char marks, about 3 minutes per side. They can also be fried on the stovetop, but they're best with a hint of charcoal. Serve warm or at room temperature.

16

Everyday Etiquette for Aliens

I took a post-graduate course in cross-cultural studies years ago (you have no idea how many degrees one has to get before spending an entire career writing about things like Boeuf Bourguignon and the importance of making your bed). I wish more of the content had stuck; alas, unless you're actually in Hong Kong or Buenos Aires or wherever, witnessing on a daily basis how people greet one other and drink their tea, it all sort of goes in one ear and out the other. What I do remember from that programme was an interesting exercise that illustrated very cleverly what a minefield any social situation can be to the uninitiated. We were tasked with explaining to an imaginary alien, who had been invited to someone's house for dinner, all the steps he'd have to take to get into the house and to the table.

Hands shot up fast. "First you show up on time," someone offered. Obvs. Well, not so obvious actually, because to be told to come at, say, eight may mean "on the dot" in Denmark, but certainly not in

France, and who only knows in the Middle East. Furthermore, where do you show up? At the door? Well, which one, might wonder our poor, bewildered creature from outer space, if there's more than one door, and, for that matter, why not through a window if you spot one that's conveniently located and wide open? On it went, as we attempted to get the alien into the house and through the meal without slapping his hostess on the back, stealing the spot at the head of the table, and eating straight out of the soup tureen. The point of the exercise was to show the extent to which we take for granted the meticulous details that govern our behaviour in daily life. It also proved that even those who claim the rules of etiquette mean nothing to them in fact have as many social boundaries as the next guy.

It's not surprising that the teacher used a dinner scenario to drive the lesson home. The dining table is, after all, one of life's great testing grounds of character and competence. I remember a late, great aunt of mine, whose career led her to the position of superintendent of schools somewhere in Connecticut, telling me that she never hired anyone until, as the last stage of the interview process, she'd taken them out for lunch. If some key character trait of the questionable sort had gone under her radar up to that point, it was bound to slip out some time between the shrimp cocktail starter and the long espresso.

Mealtimes are a key space for sussing out identity and temperament in any culture. A taxi driver once told me that an Arab expression used to determine whether a person knows someone or not is to ask, "Have you dined with him?" A conversation might go something like this:

Q: Do you know John Smith?
A: Yes.

Q: Have you dined with him?
A: No.

The "no" is the giveaway. If you haven't dined with Mr. Smith then there's no way you could possibly know him. At best you may be an acquaintance, or maybe you merely know of him; either way, if you haven't dined with him, your opinion of the person is relatively meaningless. It certainly makes sense to me, because at a table you're under the gaze of people at close quarters for extended periods of time, during which a huge number of skills get pulled into play (or not), so there's a lot to observe and draw conclusions from: you have to show up, be presentable, ask for things, eat and drink, make conversation, share, keep the peace, thank adequately.

In Emily Post's great tome *Etiquette in Society, in Business, in Politics, and at Home*, she quotes a Boston journalist as having written, "One knows the very nature of both man and woman by their actions at the table. One suddenly sees their innermost characters, their attitudes, their breeding, but above all, one knows whether one cares to spend another evening at the table with them." I found another telling quote from someone called "Agagos" (1834): "Nothing indicates a well-bred man more than a proper mode of eating his dinner . . . A man may pass muster by dressing well, and may sustain himself tolerably in conversation, but if he is not perfectly 'au fait', dinner will betray him."

Terrifying, what?

Well, according to Margaret Visser, if we happen to be hosting at the same time, the stakes are even higher. In her book *The Rituals of Dinner*, she writes, "If you are the host, your house is on view; your food (offered as the result of your best efforts) is open to judgement; your taste, your social connections, your ability to manage are all potentially 'on the line.'" The moral of the story is that if you don't want to give someone the privilege of knowing you, don't dine with them—and certainly don't invite them to dine at your house. On the other hand, if you do want to get to know someone and be known by them, an invitation to dinner is your "open sesame." This is especially true if you invite them into your own house.

Perhaps nobody understands the power of dining better than diplomats. Their careers pivot on their ability to build trusting relationships, and quickly, because those posts last only a few years. You have to get in there—sometimes into a country you've never been to before—and gain allies fast if you ever hope to make anything happen. Hospitality is one of the key ways diplomats do this. ("La gastronomie c'est l'arme de la diplomatie," as they say.)

I once met a Canadian ambassador who, under a prime minister who shall remain nameless, said he lost the most important arrow in his diplomatic quiver when word came down from on high that budgets for entertaining at home were being slashed. Senior diplomats would suddenly be required to entertain primarily by taking people to restaurants (like where, you have to wonder, the Marriott?). The results, according to my source, were catastrophic. A restaurant, you see, is both neutral turf and public arena. The walls have ears and you're not even the real boss in that situation, whereas opening up your personal space and sharing it, along with your own food, demonstrates vulnerability and provides a safe place in which to speak, which paves the road to trust much more quickly and concretely. The ambassador told me that before this new edict had come down, having people to his house for dinner meant that afterwards he could pick up the phone and call them any time for all kinds of help. Not so after he'd lost that privilege and was exiled to restaurant entertaining.

Once upon a time, I thought I wanted to be a diplomat myself. As a child I'd read the diaries of Charles Ritchie, a famous wartime diplomat, and that got the fire stoked. Then I met a number of people from the foreign service along life's way, all of whom further fueled my imagination with tales of their careers in far-flung places. Obviously, I didn't end up taking that route, which in retrospect is a good thing, because I'm too free-spirited to live in that bridled kind of world, and I don't have a natural interest in current affairs. Mind you, if a significant part of diplomacy involves entertaining, then perhaps I've done my bit. And so I shall carry on, without regret, as High Commissioner of Casa Mia, gathering friends and aliens alike, and dedicating my life to connecting people and keeping the peace, one dinner party at a time.

Chickpea Blinis with Salmon Roe

Of course, you can make regular blinis or even buy them, but these are a good (and tasty!) alternative for anyone who avoids wheat. Make the batter a few hours ahead of cooking, then fry as many blinis as you want to serve, refrigerating any remaining batter to fry another day. A dinner-party hors d'oeuvre staple in our house.

MAKES ABOUT 30

FOR THE BLINIS

1 cup/125 g chickpea flour

1 cup/250 ml water

2 tablespoons oil, plus more for frying

1 egg

1 teaspoon salt

FOR THE TOPPING

Sour cream

Salmon roe

Fresh dill sprigs, for garnish

To make the blini batter, a few hours before cooking, whisk together the flour, water, oil, egg, and salt. Pour the batter into a measuring cup or good pouring jug, and set aside. (As it sits, the batter will lose any raw chickpea taste.)

To fry the blinis (best done as close to serving as possible), heat oil in a hot pan and, working in batches, cook 2-inch/5-cm pancakes until covered in tiny pinholes all over top, about a minute. Flip, and cook the other side, then remove to paper towel to absorb any excess oil.

When all the pancakes are done, top each with a teaspoonful each of sour cream and roe. Garnish with dill, and serve.

Lamb Navarin

A crowd-pleasing spring stew, at once comforting and light, and ideal for climates like the one I live in, where March can bring some of the worst of the annual blizzards, and where no self-respecting asparagus would dream of poking its head through the ground as early as April. Serve with a bowl of buttered, parslied Yukon Gold potatoes for soaking up the juices. Note that the bouquet garni required below should be about six thyme springs, six parsley sprigs, and a bay leaf, tied together with kitchen twine.

SERVES 8

4 pounds/1.8 kg lamb shoulder, with bone if possible, trimmed of excess fat

Salt and pepper

2 tablespoons oil

1 large onion, thickly sliced

½ cup/125 ml white wine

1 tablespoon tomato paste

1 cup/250 ml chopped canned tomatoes

4 cups/1 litre cold water

1 bouquet garni (see headnote)

8 slender carrots, peeled

2 celery ribs, thickly sliced on the diagonal

1¼ pounds/560 g small turnips, peeled and cut into wedges

1 head of garlic, cloves peeled

2 cups/250 g fresh or frozen peas

Chopped fresh flat-leaf parsley, tarragon, and chives, for garnish

Continued on the next page

Heat the oven to 250°F/120°C. Trim the lamb shoulder and cut into chunks, keeping the bone. Pat the meat dry, and season with salt and pepper.

Heat the oil in a medium Dutch oven and, working in batches, brown the meat on all sides, removing as you go. Next, fry the onion until soft and browned, about 15 minutes. Deglaze the pan with the wine to get up the good bits, add the tomato paste for a minute, then add the tomatoes, water, and bouquet garni. Put the meat back in, along with the bone. Bring to a boil, skimming off any scum that rises to the surface, then cover and transfer to the oven for 1½ hours.

When the stew comes out of the oven, remove the bone and add the carrots, celery, turnips, and garlic. Return to the oven until the vegetables are cooked al dente, about 45 minutes. You can prepare the stew to this point up to a day or even two ahead of time.

When it's time to eat, skim any fat from the surface of the stew if it has sat overnight, and gently reheat, uncovered, so that the juices cook down somewhat and the vegetables soften to your liking. Add the peas just long enough to cook through. Sprinkle with herbs before serving.

17

The Business of Lunch

At some time during the pandemic, it was reported that the French were planning to lift a labour-code ban on lunching in places dedicated to work. This would mean that, for safety reasons, an exception would be made to allow people to eat at, say, their desks. Well, quelle horreur! I hope it was only temporary. I've always relied on the French to uphold standards when it comes to dining, and it would be a great disappointment if they were to fail me now. Several people for whom a proper lunch during the working day was always sacrosanct come to mind, and if you think I'm crazy to be endorsing such a practice, it is they who are to blame for the brainwashing.

One friend who worked in the wine business in Beaune used to boast that every day her boss's husband would produce lunch for all the employees, which, at the appointed hour, they would break from work to enjoy around a big wooden table in the kitchen: coq au vin one day, a variety of quiches the next, oeufs en meurette and a large salad another . . . I myself know a couple who had a real-estate business in Paris with a dining room in their office. No, not a boardroom with a table in it where you were allowed to take your plastic box of maki rolls, but an actual dining room with proper furniture, linens, and china. Every day, the wife set the table and made lunch for the whole office, or at least for those who weren't going out, and afterwards, they'd go back to their desks and carry on selling châteaux and manor houses, along with the belle vie that goes with them. You have to admit, there would be something reassuring about buying through people who so genuinely walk their own talk. (Lunch always included wine, needless to say.)

In my early days in France, witnessing such dedication to lunch made a huge impression on me, because I come from a culture in which taking virtually any kind of break is viewed with suspicion. Well, that stance got knocked out of me fast, beginning with an incident I'll never forget. I'd got a job with a luxury travel company that involved having to reconnoiter trips before they took place. My role was to venture out and vet all the starred hotels, restaurants, and cultural visits on the itinerary and make sure everything was up to snuff and organized: a visit to the Bayeux tapestries, a walk through a medieval town, a tasting at a winery, and so on. It was a fine job, but a hectic one because the full schedule of a weeklong trip would have to be squeezed into just a couple days. One such trip was to Brittany, and I was to drive there from Burgundy with a young Frenchman called, if memory serves, Sébastien. It was a long trek to get there, something like eight hours, and being still fairly new to France at the time I had not yet shed my North American belief that stopping to smell roses was supposed to be a waste of time. I was all about the destination in those days.

We got up early and were well on our way by lunchtime. If it were me doing that same trip today, we'd have been stopping somewhere in the Loire Valley for perhaps a salad of shaved garden vegetables and a nice little fish dish in cream sauce washed down with a Chenin Blanc. But, back then, it was another me behind the wheel, and I was concerned about the hands on the clock. When our stomachs began to growl, we pulled into one of those godawful roadside outlets where you can gas up, pee, and procure for yourself something like the world's most disgusting sandwich. As we were walking into the soulless joint, I said to Sébastien, "We'll just eat in the car, right?" He shrugged in apparent indifference, made his order, and headed back outside. I ordered something that would be easy to eat with just one hand and followed behind, but as I approached the car, there was no Sébastien. Where could he have gone? Then, as I got closer, I realized that he was in fact in the car, only he was in the backseat with a sort of airplane table pulled down from out of the back of the driver's seat and his lunch set upon it. "What are you doing?" I asked, completely baffled, and he, just as baffled, replied, "I thought you said you wanted to eat in the car." It hadn't even occurred to him that I'd meant, "while driving."

Later, when I worked for Anne Willan at Château du Feÿ, every meal was considered part of our training, and some of my fondest memories are of the lunches outside in summer. You couldn't possibly call them "lazy" (Anne was a workhorse who kept to a strict schedule and demanded same of all in her employ), but they were certainly bucolic and civilized. There was a terrace just outside the kitchen door, edged with stone pots of fresh herbs, and with a large table shaded by a white awning with scalloped edges. When you were lucky enough to be seated on the best side of it, you dined with a magnificent view of the Yonne Valley stretching off into the distance over fields of poppies and rapeseed.

Lunch was always at one P.M. sharp, which meant we'd all had a good four hours of work under our belts (seven, when her cooking school was in operation), mine usually in the library and some others in the kitchen. The routine was always the same: food was spread out on a buffet and we helped ourselves then found a place at the table. Constants were a giant salad, made with greens grown in the walled garden (we always had to wash them at least three times, so garden fresh—complete with slugs and dirt—they were) and a giant cheese platter groaning with favourites such as well-aged mimolette, perhaps a pyramid of chèvre, a Comté fruité, and a slice of Brie de Meaux with generous love handles. Bread, of course, was a given, and the best was that made by a master baker who sometimes brought loaves from his bakery, raw and risen, to bake in the château's wood oven located in one of the outbuildings. Crisp-crusted, soft-crumbed heaven. To round out those midday feasts, there were things like zucchini-flower frittatas, sliced melons from Provence sprinkled with crème de cassis, platters of charcuterie, bubbling gratins designed to use up an excess of Swiss chard. We'd even try oddball experiments like acacia blossoms, picked from the trees in the lane, dipped in batter, deep-fried, and drizzled with clover honey. Afterwards, we'd all help clear the scene away, then we'd get back to work in our respective corners, fully restored, and carry on until six o'clock. After just a few months of being exposed to this lunching technique, I'd started to think of it as normal, which is why, after my first year in France when I spent the winter working in New York City, I was in for a shock.

I'd got a job as a writer on an internet start-up billed as destined to become the Amazon of food websites. It was headed by a prominent food writer of the day and employed a number of budding foodies, including me, to create content, which they wanted thick and fast. I was no stranger to hard work, because, as I've said, Anne was a taskmaster, but she also practised what she preached about food and, when it came to mealtimes, I had come to expect this consistency. She knew that to think straight and perform well, you had to have a decent break at lunch, or, as Virginia Woolf put it, "One cannot think well, love well, sleep well, if one has not dined well." In the offices of that gastronomic Mount Olympus to be, I watched my colleagues with slack-jawed amazement. They seldom left the building. All morning long they guzzled coffee from mugs the size of thermoses. At noon, they'd order takeout and eat from the boxes. By nine at night (I am not exaggerating), these martyrs to the glory of all things gourmet were still at their desks, by then pouring sleeves of roasted, salted peanuts down their gullets to tide them over until . . . until what? Did they ever actually sit down at a proper table and have a meal? I never found out. I put myself on a schedule that involved arriving at the office a few hours before anyone else, so I could be out of there at a reasonable hour, and, in any case, by spring I'd moved back to France. I did later learn that the website destined to become the authority on how to eat never materialized. You have to wonder how it might have gone if it had embraced the concept of a civilized and restorative lunch.

A Summery Shrimp Salad

This pretty salad, which can also be made using lobster, takes only about fifteen lazy minutes to assemble and makes a terrific lunch worthy of cracking open a bottle of rosé.

SERVES 4

8 ounces/225 g cherry tomatoes

Salt and pepper

1 pound/450 g peeled, deveined shrimp

2 large handfuls of fresh coriander leaves (about 2 cups, loosely packed)

4 tablespoons finely chopped fresh flat-leaf parsley

2 tablespoons chopped fresh chives

2 to 3 garlic cloves, minced or crushed

2 small Thai red chili peppers, seeded and minced

Juice of 1 lime (about 3 tablespoons)

¼ cup/60 ml olive oil

Four small handfuls of arugula, for serving

Fleur de sel, for garnish

Halve the tomatoes and put them in a large bowl. Season with salt and pepper, and set aside for about 10 minutes to let the juices run.

Bring a pot of water to a boil, add the shrimp, and cook until tender, 2 to 3 minutes. Drain, and rinse in cold water. Cut the shrimp in half lengthwise, and add them to the tomatoes, along with the herbs.

Mix a dressing using the garlic, chili peppers, lime juice, and olive oil. Season, pour over the shrimp mixture, and toss well.

Scatter the arugula on a platter. Spill the shrimp mixture over top, sprinkle with some fleur de sel, and serve.

Spinach and Mushroom Tart in a Polenta Crust

An excellent lunch dish that the gluten-free can enjoy. Serve with a salad.

MAKES ONE 9-INCH/23-CM TART

FOR THE CRUST

2¼ cups/300 ml water

½ teaspoon salt

1 tablespoon olive oil or butter

¾ cup/135 g polenta

FOR THE FILLING

1 to 2 tablespoons olive oil, divided

3 slices bacon, sliced into lardons

1 shallot or small onion, minced

5 ounces/140 g button mushrooms, thinly sliced, then roughly chopped

3 ounces/90 g spinach

½ cup/40 g grated Gruyère cheese or aged white cheddar

½ cup/20 g finely grated Parmesan cheese

3 eggs

1 cup/250 ml cream (or ½ cup/125 ml each cream and milk)

¾ teaspoon salt

Freshly ground pepper

Heat the oven to 350°F/180°C. Have a 9-inch/23-cm tart shell with removable bottom at the ready.

For the crust, put the water in a saucepan and bring to a boil. Add the salt

Continued on the next page

and oil, then, whisking, add the polenta in a thin stream. Switch to a wooden spoon and cook, stirring over medium-low heat, until thick and soft, about 8 minutes. Pour into the tart pan and let sit until it's firm enough to be worked with, 5 to 10 minutes. Press into the pan like pastry to create a "crust," lay the tart pan on a baking sheet, and set aside.

For the filling, heat half the oil in a sauté pan and fry the bacon until cooked, but not crisp. Remove to paper towel to drain. Adding more oil to the pan only if needed, gently sauté the shallot until soft, then remove and scatter evenly over the base of the tart shell. Add the remaining oil and fry the mushrooms, until soft. Remove and scatter evenly over the base of the tart shell, along with the bacon. Add the spinach to the pan, cover, and wilt, 2 to 3 minutes. Remove and scatter over the base of the tart shell. Finally, scatter both cheeses evenly over the tart. Beat together the eggs and cream. Season with the salt, add pepper to taste, and pour over the filling ingredients. Bake until set and golden, about 40 minutes. Serve warm or at room temperature.

18

Share and Share Alike

Long ago in the south of France, I met a châtelaine who insisted that the recipes of her house remain secret. "If you share them with people, then everywhere you go you end up getting the same food. It's a bore." That seemed exaggerated. I mean, in what sounds like her relatively small social circle, perhaps she had a point, but I myself have always been happy to give recipes to anyone who wants them. No two people ever make a recipe in quite the same way, and, besides, isn't the whole point to pass them on? They're not personal property; they're patrimony, community glue. Or, as a Romanian friend once said of a recipe she gave me, "It's not my recipe, it belongs to my people!"

I did find the châtelaine's idea of every house having its own unique repertoire an inspiring one. Even when people own the same cookbooks or buy the same food magazines, they tend to gravitate towards different things in them, which means that each household's collection of tear sheets ends up being one-of-a kind. These rattle-bags of recipes get further shaken up with the addition of recipe hand-me-downs. Mine includes things like Aunt Etha's Cake, Jennifer's Carpaccio using the citrus fruit cédrat, Jill's Curried Consommé Cups, Luiza's Cauliflower Squares, and Isabelle's Milk Tart. You can tell at a glance that these didn't all come from the same source, but they mingle quite happily together in my recipe box, like guests at a cocktail party.

I started collecting recipes as soon as I could hold a pencil and, as hard evidence proves, before I could actually spell. The first I ever wrote down, probably around age five, was from *Sesame Street*. There was a song about, I now realize, "Indian Bannock Dough," during which a scene was shown of women in early Acadian garb using a wooden paddle to slide tiny loaves of bread into an outdoor brick oven. "Pour in flour, add a little water . . . ," went the perky ditty, as the women were shown kneading and shaping their dough. When they pulled those perfect, round, golden loaves out of the oven, I loved the look so much that I immediately wrote the recipe down on an index card: "Idiomatic doh: flor, water." It gets worse: I then attempted to make it.

No grown-ups were about, for some reason; perhaps they were all outside. I got my little brother to help drag a sack of flour out of hiding, along with the pail-sized base of a bread mixer, and we set about our project, alternating between adding flour and water and stirring with all our might, as we waited for the mixture magically to turn into dough just like on TV. Eventually, someone walked in and put a horrified stop to the operation, though I can't say I remember getting into huge trouble, instead just being given a rather stern explanation that bread requires other ingredients, such as yeast. Well, it wasn't my fault if those ladies on *Sesame Street* hadn't said so in their song.

My mother has always been an avid local historian, and for years of my youth she was researching a book that involved driving all over the community interviewing old people. She used to take me with her, I'm not sure why, and I'd wait patiently while she sat with her tape recorder asking them for facts and stories from days of old. Occasionally, I'd pipe in and get a recipe out of one of them, say for the ginger thins I'd been given for a snack to ward off restlessness. That's how I learned that everyone has a story, and everyone has a recipe.

As a teenager, I made a family cookbook, typing up all the recipes we made at home, along with some from my grandmothers and others close to the family. Some I couldn't live without to this day, such as my mother's recipes for fish chowder and oatmeal brown bread. A few I doubt I'll make again, but it doesn't matter, I'm hanging on to them for the memories. There's the family friends' recipe for "Slush," which takes me back to movie nights at their house long ago: 1 bottle cranberry cocktail, 1 can orange juice concentrate, 1 can pink lemonade concentrate, 1 juice can water, 1 quart vodka. Freeze, then mix half and half in a glass with 7 Up. There's my father's recipe for "Camel Turds," a rather leaden health-food cookie from the seventies containing, amongst other things, honey, carob chips, coconut flakes, whole wheat and soy flours, sunflower seeds, and peanuts. I never liked them, but they are symbolic of the long car trips we used to take every summer to visit my grandparents in Cape Breton. Camel Turds and comic books were what kept us children busy—and my father sane—for the nine-hour drive.

The last time I was home, one of my nieces proudly showed me a notebook she's just started containing all the recipes she's learned so far: Aunt Etha's Cake, Chocolate Duck . . . "This book could be mine!" I thought, leafing through it with a nostalgic thrill. Then, in the turn of a page, she detoured: kimchi pancake, bibimbap . . . Her mother is Korean, so already her budding collection is completely unique, with recipes from maternal and paternal sides intermingling like genes. And, pretty soon, recipes from her friends, travels, and experiences will join the assembly, each one a Polaroid of a moment in her life, each one waiting for its turn to receive the honour of being passed on.

Molasses Snaps

It took me years to get this recipe out of a Nova Scotian friend, who, in turn, had to get it out of his grandmother. These are crisp, thin, buttery, and delicious with a cup of tea.

MAKES 65 TO 75 COOKIES

1 cup/225 g butter, softened

⅓ cup/75 g sugar

⅔ cup/150 ml molasses

2½ cups/310 g flour

½ teaspoon ground ginger

1 teaspoon ground cinnamon

½ teaspoon salt

½ teaspoon baking soda

Cream together the butter and sugar, then mix in the molasses until smooth. Sift together the flour, ginger, cinnamon, salt, and baking soda; then combine with the molasses mixture to make a smooth dough. Shape the dough into 2 logs, about 2-inches in diameter. Wrap in parchment, and chill for a few hours until firm enough to slice very thin.

Heat the oven to 350°F/180°C. Working in batches, slice the dough into disks about ¼ inch/6 mm thick. Lay the cookies on a large parchment-lined baking sheet, set somewhat apart (they spread a bit). Bake until set, about 10 minutes, keeping an eye on them as they can burn easily.

Remove from the oven and cool. Store in an airtight container.

Cauliflower Squares

This is an unusual recipe based on one from a Romanian friend who serves her savoury squares with drinks. They involve roasted cauliflower held together by a tangy custard of yoghurt, cream, and cheeses, all flavoured with dill and seductively mild heat. I love having a pan of them hanging around the kitchen to snack on. Cut into larger pieces, they also make a nice, light lunch, served with salad.

SERVES 8

1 medium cauliflower (about 1½ pounds/675 g)

Olive oil, for drizzling

Salt and pepper

3 eggs, at room temperature

1 cup/250 ml yoghurt

½ cup/125 ml sour cream

¼ cup/10 g finely grated Parmesan cheese

1½ teaspoons onion powder

A pinch of chili pepper flakes

5 ounces/140 g feta, grated on a box grater (about 1 cup)

A large handful of chopped fresh dill (about 1 loosely packed cup)

½ cup/30 g grated Gruyère or aged cheddar

Smoked paprika, for sprinkling

A handful of chopped fresh chives

Heat the oven to 450°F/230°C.

Core the cauliflower and cut it into florets. Spread on a baking sheet. Drizzle with a little olive oil, and season with salt and pepper. Roast until tender and golden, about 15 minutes. Remove from the oven, cool completely, and roughly chop.

While the cauliflower cooks, beat the eggs very well with a whisk, then beat in the yoghurt, sour cream, Parmesan cheese, onion powder, and chili pepper flakes. Allow to come to room temperature so that the mixture is pourably liquid. Season with salt and pepper.

When the cauliflower is done, remove from the oven and turn the heat down to 400°F/200°C. Line an 8-inch/20-cm baking pan with parchment paper, and grease with a little olive oil.

Spread half the cauliflower over the bottom of the pan, sprinkle over the feta and dill, followed by half the Gruyère, then top with the remaining cauliflower. Spoon the egg mixture evenly over, then scatter the remaining Gruyère evenly over the top, and lightly press with a spatula to flatten the top. Sprinkle with the paprika and chives, and bake until set, 25 to 30 minutes. Cool to room temperature and cut into squares to serve.

19

Recipe for Life

One nice thing about moving house is that it makes you look at the things around you with the eye of a gardener going after weeds. Not that I have any immediate plans to move house, but at some level of my psyche the seed of desire to do so must have taken root, because lately I find myself mentally labelling objects "to take" and "to leave." I'm tempted, in fact, to start getting rid of anything in the "to leave" category already. Why live with things if we don't really love them, and why especially if we don't even need them? Then I found myself wondering which objects I'll choose to surround myself with when the day comes that a somewhat shrunken version of myself decides it wants no more space to worry about than one or two rooms. The capsule Laura, if you will, what will it consist of: a shawl, a teacup, a few family photographs, a silver vase of peonies? Continuing to travel on that train of thought, my mind then rattled on towards the question of what, if reduced to only an essential handful, the recipes of my life would be.

One of the first "recipes" ever to hold any real emotional weight for me was for fried potato skins. My mother used to make these for us after baked potato lunches when we'd been particularly well behaved. Having obediently emptied our skins of their creamy flesh, my brothers and I would slice them and scrape them clean with the skillfulness of trappers, then we'd arrange our pelts on plates and admire our handiwork while waiting for our mother to melt butter into a sizzling froth in the cast-iron pan. In went the skins to fry until crisp, then they received a sprinkling of salt and were returned to us like a prize. Fried potato skins were something I instinctively handled daintily and always savoured slowly, like the little girl in a book I had who always went to school with a white linen napkin in her lunchbox. Unlike the other kids on the playground who ran around with their peanut-butter sandwiches, this little lady sat on a bench with her napkin in her lap and ate things like hot tomato soup from a thermos or a cold chicken leg. I thought she was too sophisticated for words, and perhaps nibbling at fried potato skins like a lady made me feel I was living a little closer to her gold standard.

There's a dish Peter tells me he finds quintessentially "Laura," and funnily he's the only person who could ever say so because he's the only person, apart from myself, that I ever serve it to. It's a recipe—more of a way of cooking, actually—that seems naturally to flow from my hands when I'm in the kitchen alone. I make it in a copper sauté pan, which, if we were going to play a round of desert-island-kitchen-equipment, would certainly be on my list. First, I fry some bacon pieces, then I set those aside while I sauté a mirepoix in olive oil. Once that's soft, I add garlic and chili peppers, then a bit of tomato paste, bay leaf, thyme, and white wine. The calm, gradual process of the whole thing has the dish and me constantly interacting, keeping each other company. That's part of its charm. Now in go chicken stock and lentils. I stir those occasionally as they simmer away, and once the lentils are tender, I season with salt and pepper, add a handful of chopped parsley, another of grated Parmesan cheese, and finally the afore-fried bacon. The result is a thick, smoky, healthy stew, which to me is perfect food, the kind of thing I'm desperate for particularly after travel when I've been delighted-out by exotica.

I had a professor of social psychology in university who constantly repeated a couplet from Robbie Burns, "Oh wad some pow'r the giftie gie us. To see oursels as ithers see us." (Oh would some power the gift give us, to see ourselves as others see us.) I don't know that I ever really understood what he was trying to drive home until years later, when I saw myself on television. Of course, I knew it was me, but it was also a stranger I was watching, one who pronounced words in ways I was completely oblivious to and who gestured and moved in ways that came as a total surprise. It's very difficult to put a finger on our own traits and styles, because they're too much a part of us, and it's impossible to see ourselves through the eyes of others.

Perhaps some who saw me cook on TV might cite as a typical Laura recipe something more along the lines of Butter Lettuce Salad with Flowers and Foie Gras, from my cookbook *Paris Express*. It was inspired by a long-ago meal in a hole-in-the-wall in the seventh arrondissement, and I don't know how my friends and I ever found the place, because it did little to draw attention to itself, which must explain why we were the only ones in there that night. One man alone was running the dining room; his wife, it turned out, was the cook. He took no individual orders, but simply served the table what was coming out of the kitchen: first, a giant bowl of salad with generous chunks of foie gras tossed throughout; next, duck confit and fried potatoes; and finally, an entire apple tart. We dragged the meal out over more than a couple of bottles of wine, and I still remember it as one of the most magical meals I ever had in Paris. The foie gras salad I later came up with bears no resemblance to the one we had that night, but I still make the association. To mine, I added tarragon and chives, pine nuts and edible flower petals. I used Champagne vinegar in the dressing, and thinly sliced foie gras instead of chunks. I love rusticity, but somehow I always seem to want to move in and pretty it up a bit. You might say the effect on any recipe in my hands is like the effect on the average bachelor's living arrangements after acquiring a wife: they're given a feminine touch. (Just ask Peter what happened to his place when I first moved in with him!)

Having just said that, I wonder if that "touch" isn't, in fact, my ultimate recipe. Rather than narrowing it down to one specific dish, perhaps it's a person's recipe for life that counts. Ingredients: love and care. Method: make it nice. I apply this recipe even to something like a boiled egg. It must be farm fresh, lowered gently into boiling water, simmered for nine minutes, refreshed in icy water, peeled smooth, halved, and laid on a plate, perhaps dribbled with brown butter for a bit of luxury, and garnished with an herb. It's a recipe you can apply to every moment of your life, really. I hope I'll remember that if the day ever comes when I'm down to one or two rooms, sitting at a table, rifling through old photographs, with no company other than myself, a vase of peonies, and a cup of tea.

Hot and Smoky Lentil Stew

This is the kind of warming, satisfying food I make when I'm not following a recipe, so feel comfortable treating these instructions in a loosey-goosey way. If you're looking for a thick soup to eat with crusty bread, use 3 cups of stock. For a stewier mixture to use as a base for grilled sausage, torn bits of duck confit, perhaps a piece of cod or a fried egg, use only 2 cups.

SERVES 4 TO 6

4 tablespoons olive oil, divided

2 slices/2 ounces/60 g bacon, cut into pieces

1 cup/100 g finely diced celery (about 1 fat rib)

1 cup/140 g finely diced carrot (about 1 large)

1 cup/140 g finely chopped onion (about 1 medium)

Salt and pepper

3 garlic cloves, minced

1 tablespoon tomato paste

¼ teaspoon chili pepper flakes

Pinch of saffron threads

1 bay leaf

1 strip of orange peel

1 heaping tablespoon chopped fresh thyme

½ cup/125 ml white wine

1 cup/250 ml crushed tomatoes

2 to 3 cups/500 to 750 ml fish stock

1 cup/175 g cooked lentils, plus more to taste

A handful of finely chopped fresh flat-leaf parsley

Freshly grated Parmesan cheese, for garnish

Put half the oil in a cold sauté pan with the bacon. Turn on the heat, and gently fry the bacon until cooked, but not crisp. Remove with a slotted spoon, leaving the fat in the pan, and set aside. Add the remaining oil and the celery and fry for 5 minutes. Add the carrot and onion, season with salt and pepper, and continue cooking until all the vegetables are tender, about 15 minutes more.

Now, add the garlic, tomato paste, chili pepper flakes, saffron, bay leaf, orange peel, and thyme, stirring for a minute. Put the bacon back in. Pour in the wine, crushed tomatoes, and stock, bring to a simmer, cover, and cook gently for 20 minutes. Stir in the lentils and parsley, and simmer a further 5 minutes. Taste and adjust the seasonings. Remove the bay leaf and orange peel. Serve hot with a drizzle of olive oil and some Parmesan.

Spring Vegetable Ragout
with Shaved Ham

A colourful tangle of new vegetables is a most welcome sight in spring, ideal as a first course or side dish. The vegetables are variable (I love adding pattypan squash to the mix in summer), so feel free to mix them up. Just be sure to add them to the pan in order of longest cooking to shortest so that everything finishes at the same time. Be aware that this is also excellent with a few glugs of heavy cream added at the end and left to bubble a bit to heat through and thicken.

SERVES 4

¼ cup/60 g butter

6 morel mushrooms, halved lengthwise

1 small leek, trimmed and sliced

4 small carrots, halved lengthwise (about 4 ounces/110 g)

4 baby turnips, or a larger one peeled and cut into wedges (about 4 ounces/110 g)

2 to 4 radishes, halved lengthwise (about 4 ounces/110 g)

Salt and pepper

1½ cups/375 ml homemade chicken stock

4 asparagus spears, peeled and halved lengthwise

½ cup/75 g freshly shelled peas

1 cup/150 g freshly podded fava beans, blanched and shelled

A handful of chopped fresh flat-leaf parsley, tarragon, and chives, for garnish

4 very thin slices Black Forest ham (about 1½ ounces/45 g)

Heat the butter in a sauté pan and fry the morels until just cooked. Remove the morels and set them aside. Next, add the leek to the pan and fry until softened. Add the carrots, turnips, and radishes, season with salt and pepper, pour in the stock, and cook until the vegetables are just shy of tender, about 10 minutes, depending on size, and the cooking liquid is reduced to jus.

Add the asparagus and peas and cook until tender, about 5 minutes longer. Finally, add the fava beans, and return the morels to the pan to heat through. Either tip onto a serving platter or divide amongst 4 plates. Scatter the herbs over the vegetables, and drape the ham on top. Serve.

20

Taming the Beast

The first time I ever saw an artichoke was the summer before my last year of high school, which I spent in Quebec working as an au pair for a French family to improve my language skills. One day I walked into the kitchen and there was little "Caro," the three-year-old in my charge, sitting before some reptilian-looking green thing on a plate. She peeled off its giant scales, one by one, dipped them in melted butter, then scraped the flesh off in her teeth. I watched her perform this at once delicate and savage operation until all the scales were gone. Then she picked up her fork and finished the beast off by tucking into its "heart." She was as blasé handling that artichoke as I, at the same age, could only have been with an apple.

It wasn't until years later, in France, that this daunting thistle would gradually become a familiar food to me, too. It was one of Anne Willan's staple starters: tight, fresh globe artichokes from Brittany, first boiled, then filled to the brim with hollandaise sauce. We were all expected to be able to make them practically blindfolded. A good bread knife, we learned, was best for sawing off the tops. Next, you trimmed the bases by pulling off any excess leaves and running a paring knife around the edge to clean things up. Immediately, you rubbed any cut parts with lemon so they didn't turn brown. Once the artichokes had been boiled in citrusy water, and were cool enough to handle, we lifted out their fleshless centre leaves, then gingerly scraped out the Muppet-stiff hairs at the base of the "wells," which protect the prized hearts. We set the ready artichokes upside down on a tea towel so that any water hiding in the crevices could drain out while we prepared the sauce. The hollandaise, it turned out, was even more formidable a task than preparing the artichokes, or it seemed so back then. These days I find it no more difficult than whisking up a mayonnaise, which is essentially what a hollandaise is, albeit a warm version, made with butter instead of oil.

The word "apprivoiser," meaning to tame or to domesticate, is used in St. Exupéry's *The Little Prince* in a unique and quite untranslatable way. In the story of a stranded pilot and a little boy, whose paths cross in the desert after a plane malfunction, the sense of the word is more reciprocal than one-sided. Two beings are portrayed ultimately as taming each other, in the sense that by devoting time to one another they form a bond. The Little Prince "tames" a flower, for instance, which means he takes care of it and therefore, with the flower, develops a connection. I see my English translation of the book describes "apprivoiser" as "establishing a tie." It's so much nicer than our understanding of taming as something more like conquering. I've always been fond of the word "apprivoiser" because of that.

Anyway, you'd think such a word would be reserved for relationships with things like horses and dogs or, at a stretch, perhaps even a garden. But, if you allow yourself to be romantic enough, it can apply to virtually anything at all, including ingredients and recipes. The artichoke, for example, once a complete stranger to me, has become, after much attentive interaction, a cozy companion. Ditto, more recently, Hainanese chicken rice.

I'm not sure where I first encountered this recipe, said to be one of the top dishes in the world, but at some point I got a glimpse of it and was starstruck. Perhaps YouTube started coughing up images of it under my nose, because I certainly watched enough videos about its preparation, including in languages I don't understand one syllable of. I discovered you're meant to "exercise" the bird before you begin to prepare it, to loosen the skin (chicken calisthenics, if you will). Then you massage it with salt, give it a good, cold shower, and remove as much fat as you can for melting and adding to the rice. The chicken is poached in stock that simmers so gently there's barely a ripple on the surface, and at the exact moment when it is cooked, the bird is lifted out and plunged into an ice bath to cool. Finally, it is hung from a hook, generously rubbed with sesame oil, and left to dry. How's that for a full spa treatment? No wonder it is such a pure and delicate dish. It's served with rice that has been cooked with the chicken fat, garlic, and some of the strained stock, which I mould using a small bowl and turn out into perfect mounds on a silver platter. Additional accompaniments to the chicken include fresh coriander, sliced cucumber, green onion sauce, chili sauce, and soy sauce, along with side bowls of cooking broth for sipping. It's one of those incredibly simple dishes which, at the same time, can scare the hell out you, until, of course, the recipe has been "apprivoisé."

How does a person tame a wily recipe, then? The fox who befriends the Little Prince in the story and begs to be tamed by him explains the process thus: "You must be very patient . . . First you will sit down at a little distance from me—like that—in the grass. I shall look at you out of the corner of my eye, and you will say nothing . . . But, you will sit a little closer to me, every day . . . " That was me with chicken rice on YouTube in the early stages. Every day I'd watch someone else make it, including people who had nowhere but an outdoor kitchen to cook in. It's a bit like thinking you might like to get to know someone, but you're not quite sure, and then you find out that they're actually a friend of a friend, so suddenly they seem safe. Pre-vetting emboldens a person. So, having seen that enough seemingly reliable people had been able to get chummy with the recipe, I summoned the courage to introduce myself to it as well. I even went to Chinatown and bought a special hook for hanging the chicken. Once I had that, I felt truly committed—a bit like buying a saddle and then thinking, "Well, since I have this, I might as well get a horse"—and then the trials began.

It worked fine the first time, though it was a bit stressful juggling all the parts. I figured that as long as I didn't wait too long before a second attempt, I could shake my nervous edge, which I did. Then I made it again, and again, feeling more confident every time, until, before I knew it, Hainanese chicken rice felt, perhaps not as much a part of my inner circle as an apple, but certainly as friendly an acquaintance as the once forbidding artichoke.

Hainanese Chicken Rice

It may sound plain but this dish is, in fact, a sensation: chicken gently poached in an aromatic broth until it's soft and silky, then served with chicken fat–flavoured rice, crunchy cucumber, fresh herbs, tasty sauces, and soothing bowls of hot broth on the side for sipping. It's clean, comforting, and exciting all at once, the sort of food it's impossible to tire of. This is an easy recipe, but there are a number of moving parts, so I recommend reading through from beginning to end and doing a full mise en place of ingredients before launching in. I also like to get the sauces out of the way right up front so I can give the chicken and rice my full concentration. All in all, a recipe well worth taking the time and making the effort to get to know.

SERVES 4

FOR THE CHICKEN

1 small chicken, about 3 pounds/1.4 kg, with neck and all fat still
  attached

Coarse salt

10 cups/2.5 litres light chicken stock, made from chicken stock
  powder (more if needed)

A thumb of fresh ginger, peeled and sliced

3 garlic cloves, sliced

Tops from 4 green onions, cut into pieces

Pepper

Sesame oil, for rubbing

1 English cucumber or 4 Lebanese cucumbers, sliced, for serving

1 large bunch of coriander leaves, for serving

1½ cups/330 g Thai jasmine rice

1 tablespoon oil

Reserved chicken tail and fat

1 tablespoon minced garlic

2½ cups/625 ml poaching liquid from the chicken

½ teaspoon salt

Chili Sauce (recipe follows)

Ginger and Green Onion Sauce (recipe follows)

Sweet Soy Sauce (recipe follows)

To make the chicken, first "exercise" it a bit by moving its legs around to loosen the skin. Rub all over with coarse salt, massaging gently, then rinse thoroughly. Remove the neck from the chicken and set aside for the stock. Cut the tail off the chicken and trim all excess fat from around the cavity and neck. Set these bits aside for when it's time to make the rice.

In a pot large enough to hold the bird, bring the stock to a simmer, adding the neck, along with the ginger, garlic, and green onion tops. Season with pepper. Dip the chicken in and out of the broth a few times, then submerge it completely. Cover, and poach as gently as possible for 40 minutes.

Remove the pot from the heat and leave it to sit, still covered, for a further 20 minutes for the chicken to finish cooking. It will be ready as soon as a skewer pierced into a leg shows the juices running clear. Prepare a large bowl of ice water. Transfer the chicken from the stock to the ice water for a few minutes to cool, then set on a carving board. Rub all over with sesame oil. Strain the cooking broth into a bowl, then pour it back into the pot, discarding the aromatics. Measure out the 2½ cups/625 ml of stock needed for the rice, and keep the rest warm.

While the chicken is poaching, begin the rice. First, soak it in a large bowl of cold water for 20 minutes, then rinse well, pour into a strainer, and leave in the sink or set over a bowl for 20 minutes to drain completely. Heat the oil

Continued on the next page

in a medium saucepan over low heat, and add the reserved chicken tail and fat. Cook gently until the tail is golden brown and the fat has rendered. You should have a few tablespoons of fat. Discard the tail. Add the garlic, rice, and, once the chicken has finished poaching, the reserved 2½ cups/625 ml stock and the salt. Cover and bring to a boil, then reduce to low and cook until all the stock has been absorbed, about 10 minutes. Uncover, quickly lay a clean tea towel over the pot, then replace the lid. Let sit off the heat for at least 10 minutes or until serving.

To serve, remove the legs from the chicken, then the breasts. Slice the breast meat, split the legs between thigh and drumstick, and arrange all on a platter. Place the sliced cucumber and coriander alongside. Fluff the rice and, using a small bowl, mould four mounds and turn them out onto a serving platter. Serve the chicken rice with the prepared sauces, along with bowls of the fragrant steaming-hot broth for sipping.

Chili Sauce

A welcome bit of gentle heat.

MAKES ABOUT ½ CUP/125 ML

3 long, red chilis, seeded and roughly chopped

2-inch piece of fresh ginger, peeled and sliced

3 garlic cloves, sliced

½ teaspoon salt

½ teaspoon sugar

¼ teaspoon sesame oil

Juice of ½ lime

½ teaspoon rice vinegar

2 tablespoons chicken broth

Put the chilis, ginger, garlic, salt, and sugar in a mortar and pestle and pound to a paste. (Alternatively, do this in a food processor.) Add the oil, lime juice, vinegar, and broth and mix thoroughly (or pulse to blend). You should have a thick, rough sauce. Transfer to a serving bowl.

Ginger and Green Onion Sauce

Note that this is not merely a stirring job, so do refer to the method before you start mixing.

MAKES ABOUT ½ CUP/125 ML

4 green onions, thinly sliced

2 tablespoons grated fresh ginger

Pinch of salt

Continued on the next page

¼ cup/60 ml vegetable oil

1 teaspoon sesame oil

Put the green onions, ginger, and salt in a mortar and pestle and pound to a paste. Heat the vegetable oil in a small saucepan and, once sizzling, pour it over the paste. Mix to combine, then add the sesame oil. Transfer to a serving bowl.

Sweet Soy Sauce

A bit of umami.

MAKES ABOUT ⅓ CUP/75 ML

2½ tablespoons boiling water

1½ tablespoons sugar

2½ tablespoons soy sauce

Stir together the water and sugar to dissolve, then stir in the soy sauce. Transfer to a serving bowl.

21

The Whole Point of Pleasure

I was listening to an interview the other day with a young Deepak Chopra, now a well-established New Age guru, wherein he was emphasizing the importance of pleasure when it comes to eating. Apparently, depending on one's mental and emotional state, the body metabolizes food differently, which is why he said you never want to sit down to dinner when you're stressed out. He particularly cautioned against eating when angry or dining with people we don't like (I'm sure fear would factor in, too), otherwise the body and the food going into it will be at war. In short, his message was that there can be no such thing as healthy eating if one isn't also happy.

The French, of course, have always defended the idea that dining well is essential to living well—along with dressing well, being well groomed, speaking well, and so on—but I've never heard them say why. I suppose pleasure and beauty are so engrained in the culture they simply take it for granted. But, I'm always interested to discover the reasoning behind why things are done. Good posture, I've learned, isn't merely a way of looking proper or powerful, it's essential because it's the only way the spine can function correctly. The reason waiters serve food from the left instead of the right isn't a silly, random, dining-room rule, it's so that drinking glasses, which are always positioned to the right, don't get knocked flying in the process. Chewing food properly isn't about etiquette either, but about digestion (apparently, much of the digestion process actually happens in the mouth). And, now, lo and behold, the point of pleasurable dining (i.e., eating in a relaxed and happy state, surrounded by people we enjoy, in a serene and beautiful environment) comes down not to hedonism, but, again, to prioritizing physical health.

This is all wonderful news, but it does beg the question of what to do when you can't control all these factors. What if you have to dine every night in a prison cafeteria, for example? Or, what if you've lost your job and are soon to be evicted from your flat? You can't just snap your fingers and make stress go away so that your body will perfectly digest your takeout chow mein. Even when the outside world seems hunky-dory, sometimes our inner landscapes are such that letting our appetites loose on the night seems a risky business. That is, if we even have an appetite at all.

I had this trouble a few years ago during an anxiety-riddled stretch that robbed me of hunger for several months. It wasn't such a big deal at home where nobody would know if all I ate for dinner was a peeled grape; but it was problematic at dinner parties. There everyone would be digging into glorious spreads, and I'd choke down half an inch of steak and a leaf of lettuce like I was being force-fed an entire cow and its pasture. For the rest of the evening, I'd push around with a fork whatever remained on my plate until somebody mercifully took it away. Before long, my weight had plummeted and I looked quite gaunt, not that I actually remember any of this, but there's evidence in the form of a photograph from the era that's rather shocking. Imagine a portrait of Virginia Woolf if it had been painted by Edvard Munch and you get the idea.

Peter decided it might do me good to get away to Paris for a break, which was a nice idea, but also a daunting one. I was worried I'd be a joyless travel companion because all the croissants and this-es and thats à la crème would be wasted on me. He pressed on with his plans and, for whatever reason, booked our flight through Montreal with a stopover. I guess he wanted the excuse of a few hours in his hometown and to make the getting there half the fun. We could walk up the mountain, take in a market, and peruse the shops along rue Saint-Denis before heading back to the airport and crossing the ocean. Alas, when we landed in Montreal, it was pouring rain, so any wandering around while awaiting the next flight was out of the question. Peter checked his watch: it was getting close to one, so he called L'Express, a bistro so old-school you're hard-pressed to find anything like it even in Paris. Great. Just the place to take someone with the appetite of a housefly for the entire afternoon.

Luckily, I like L'Express, so even if I ended up ordering a glass of water and an olive I guessed it would be okay. And it was indeed, right from the get-go. Reassurance greets you at the door in the form of a grown-up maître d', so you know you're in good hands. The timeless décor has an immediately comforting effect: black-and-white chequered floor, a bar the colour of bull's blood, white tablecloths at dinner, wooden bistro chairs that you're allowed to stay in for as long as you like without fear of being shooed away to make room for the next customer. Mercifully, there is no music, which in most restaurants is so loud it's like dining under an air show. Here, the only music you hear is the choir of voices having a good time.

We were given a table in the window, where the rain was scribbling illegible notes on the pane outside. We ordered kirs to sip on while we looked at the menu: céleri rémoulade, foie gras terrine, salade de betteraves, steak frites, soupe de poisson, crème caramel, mousse au chocolat . . . The tried and the true. I was debating what to order when a voice to my right suddenly said, "The tongue is absolutely delicious." It wasn't a waiter, but rather the wife of an elderly couple whose plates were just being cleared to make way for dessert. They spoke French but were originally from Lebanon, which we found out in about five minutes because, in Montreal restaurants, patrons actually talk to one another. It's not like in so many other cities where you can have a bar full of people and everyone at it staring straight ahead like blinkered horses on parade. We chatted away for a while about the glories of Beirut, and then we went back to our menus.

Eventually, I settled on sorrel soup, followed by the recommended tongue in caper sauce with a frilly salad on top. Peter chose cold roast beef with fries and mayonnaise and requested a bottle of Beaujolais. By the time we'd finished our kirs, already I felt different. It was the strangest thing. All the troubles of the past many months seemed to have lifted away, or seemed at least temporarily to have made themselves scarce. Our food arrived and, amazingly, I ate. Everything! With each bite, I kept waiting for my body to flick the internal switch that had been putting a gag reflex into action for the better part of a year, and it didn't happen. We even ordered cheese afterwards, and, as the afternoon carried on, chocolate truffles with Cognac and coffee. It was the first time I'd taken pleasure in eating for as long as I could remember. What exactly it was about that restaurant on that day that had the magic to produce such an immediate effect, I'll never know, but it worked, and not just for one lunch either. The whole time we were in Paris, I ate like good old me.

I'd be lying if I pretended that the meal at L'Express and the time in Paris were permanent cures. When I came back, of course, the lack of desire to eat and the causes behind it were there to greet me. It took proper time and effort to get back my full appetite for life, but eventually it returned. Still, the experience of that lunch did impress upon me the power that a perfect meal can have to pull back the curtain of our human woes, at least temporarily, and allow us to catch a glimpse of ourselves at our best. Even if we regress afterwards, at least we come away with an ideal to hold in our minds like a North Star, a vision of what "making it" looks like while we carry on having to fake it a little while longer.

The Skinny Beet Green Frittata

The secret here is that you're beating goat cheese thoroughly into the egg up front, rather than adding it in pinches or using grated cheese. The result is what has become one of my all-time favourite egg dishes, skinny, creamy, packed with nutritious greens, and delicious. In the absence of beet greens, spinach makes a good alternative. If you have leftovers, wrap them and refrigerate; they reheat well. A perfect lunch for a light appetite.

SERVES 2

Tops (with stems) from 3 beets, about 5 ounces/140 g of greens

4 eggs

¼ cup/60 g soft goat cheese, cream cheese, or ricotta

3 tablespoons finely grated Parmesan cheese

Salt and pepper

Pinch of cayenne pepper

Scant scrape of nutmeg

A generous knob of butter, for frying

Wash the beet greens very thoroughly, as they can be sandy. Put an inch of water in a saucepan, add the greens, cover, and cook until the stems are tender, about 8 minutes. Drain, and rinse in cold water. Spill onto a clean tea towel, then twist into a tight ball over the sink to remove the liquid. Cut into pieces, and set aside.

Beat together the eggs and soft cheese (it's okay if it stays a bit lumpy), then whisk in the Parmesan, salt and pepper, cayenne, and nutmeg. Stir the greens through with a fork.

Heat a nonstick frying pan over medium heat, and add the butter. Once it froths, pour in the egg mixture, spreading it out evenly with a spatula, and turn the heat down to low. Cook, lifting the edges of the frittata with a rubber spatula so that the wet egg can slide under and cook. When almost set, cover and continue cooking until set enough to flip. All this should take only a few minutes.

Once the top is sufficiently set, then, with the lid on, flip the pan over so the frittata lands on the lid. Slide it back into the pan so you can cook the other side for a minute. Slide onto a cutting board, and cut into wedges to serve.

Peaches with Prosciutto and Basil

Juicy, ripe peaches with salty ham, garnished with peppery leaves of basil, is summertime in a mouthful. It makes an elegant plated first course for two, but you can also opt to make a giant platter of it to set before a crowd. Effortless and irresistible.

SERVES 2

2 ripe, juicy peaches, at room temperature

4 cigarette-paper-thin slices best-quality prosciutto

About 6 basil leaves

Olive oil

Excellent balsamic vinegar (optional)

Bring a pot of water to a boil. Carve an X into the bottom of each peach and drop them in for 8 to 10 seconds. Remove, run under cold water until they're cool enough to handle, then peel, halve, pit, and slice.

Arrange the peaches on 2 serving plates and drape the prosciutto over top. Tear the basil leaves and scatter them over, then drizzle over a tiny bit of oil to make things glisten, and, only if you like, add a few drops of the vinegar. Serve.

22

Your Order, Madam?

There were too many pears, all turning ripe at the same moment, which is why I forced myself to slice one up to eat. I don't know why I bought so many. Some little voice in my head must have started nagging me with "It's autumn! Eat of the season!" and got me to fill the basket. I don't, unfortunately, have a habit of eating fruit, so though occasionally I buy it with good intentions, it usually sits around until it needs to be tossed. Noticing the ripe pears today, I decided it wasn't going to happen this time. I put a first slice in my mouth, perfectly ripe and pearfully sweet, and suddenly my whole body reacted in a manner so grateful, so relieved, it was as though it had been begging me to eat pears for decades and been denied every plea until that moment. "Yes!" my body rejoiced. "This is what I've been trying to tell you!" I gobbled down the whole fruit.

Someone from whom I've taken a great deal of advice once gave me a suggestion that I've never actually put into practice. She told me always before putting food into my mouth to ask my body, "What do you feel like eating right now?" It's not the same as looking at a menu and choosing between a mushroom risotto or a minestrone, nor is it the same as leaning on the fridge door after work and deciding you'd better finish the chicken soup tonight and save the pasta sauce for tomorrow. It's more like recognizing a craving for, say, kale, and then deliberately going out and getting it. In reverse, it's like eating a pear and then "hearing" your whole body express with great intensity, "What a relief. That's exactly what I needed."

Have you ever seen that trick where you hold up an arm, straight out to the front of you and perpendicular to the ground, then have someone ask you a yes/no question and immediately try to push down on your arm? If the arm doesn't move, your answer is affirmative, but if it falls, then you've got a big "no." Business leaders teach this sort of thing as a way of getting people to listen to their guts. Others prefer to appeal to pendulums, holding them over their open palms with a question to test for a positive (circles to the right) or a negative (circles to the left). I suppose some might even swing them over fruit bowls and dinner plates, too. "Pendulum, is this banana, this cheese, this chocolate good for me?" A bit kooky, but then so are plenty of people.

Most of the time, we're unconscious about what we put down the gullet. The morning coffee is poured and laced with cream before our eyes are even half open. A bowl of bar nuts will mysteriously vanish as we catch up with a friend at the end of the day. It's only when it's too late and the third brownie finally registers that we might wish we'd consulted with our body first. But, should we really be waiting for our body to start hollering before we're willing to lend it an ear?

I had a strange incident last summer that made me think I should perhaps start taking the "ask the body" advice seriously. I'd made a ratatouille, out of perfect vegetables as it happened, though it is a dish known to be useful for zucchinis, peppers, and aubergines that may be past their prime. Once they're all nice and soft and goopy, you never know the difference, until, even if you've used the best of vegetables, apparently you do. I served the dish to some friends about three days after making it, by which time it had already been reheated once or twice and had started to take on a slightly jammy quality. In fact, it was tasty, rich and flavoursome, and all that you could want, but I'm remembering that there was something about it that didn't feel quite right. I only realized after I'd already set it on the table: that ratatouille had no energy left in it, and my body could tell.

For years I've carried around a quote in my head, the origins of which I've forgotten: "Close thy lips that thy tongue may taste the sweetness of the mouth." I doubt it has anything to do with food, though I suppose it could be a suggestion not to eat, but to appreciate some emptiness. More likely, it's guru-ese for "listen inwards" (i.e., shut up), which, at the time of writing, I've been attempting to do all day, because my body has refused to eat anything, refused to get dressed, and refused to leave the house. This is completely unlike me, or, should I say, unlike my body.

One of the most memorable reads from my final year of undergraduate school was Milan Kundera's play *Jacques and His Master*, an homage to Diderot's *Jacques le Fataliste* and, for me at the time, a fascinating examination of the relationship between master and servant. Who is truly weak and who is truly powerful in this world? Anyone with an infant quickly learns who's boss. Well, it's sort of the same with our bodies. We're very good at bossing them around most of the time, making them head out to the office, even if coughing and shivering, or making them drink excessive litres of water even when they're not thirsty. Almost always, we let our brains drive the ship.

Well, not today. I decided to switch roles, for once, and just wait to see what would happen. My body stayed in pyjamas all morning and lay back on the sofa. It drank three teas and two hot chocolates, and half a bottle of fizzy water. "You should really eat something," Peter said to me by mid-afternoon. "No, you should not," interjected my body, alarmingly confident in its new command position. It reminded me of a story my mother tells about when, at around the age of nine months, I suddenly turned my head from her breast and refused to drink ever again. Something must not have agreed with me, though she claims I was just being stubborn. Either that, or my infant brain was thinking, "Isn't it time I was given a crystal coupe?"

Now, the day is almost done, and Peter is making turkey soup. It actually smells appealing, filling the whole house with the scent of reassurance and giving me the first hint of an appetite all day. To be sure, I've just made a discreet internal enquiry . . . and my body says okay, so serve it forth!

Green and White Chicken (or Turkey) Soup

The best chicken soup in the world is inevitably the one you grew up with, which is longhand for saying that this is my mother's recipe. Time and attentiveness are unlisted yet key ingredients, so, although this soup is simple and doesn't take very long to make, it's best to start it early in the day so it can take its time mellowing into its healing, soothing self. I know there are many types of chicken soup in the world, each delicious in its own way, but this, without alteration, is the one I want when I'm having an I-need-my-mummy kind of day.

SERVES 6

8 cups/2 litres unsalted homemade chicken or turkey stock

1 teaspoon salt

Freshly ground pepper

5 celery ribs, minced (about 3 cups)

3 tablespoons chopped fresh thyme leaves

1 very large onion, minced (about 3 cups)

2 cups/30 g loosely packed fresh flat-leaf parsley leaves, finely chopped

3 large garlic cloves, minced

1 to 2 teaspoons chicken stock powder

About 2 cups/250 g shredded cooked chicken or turkey

About 2 cups/500 g cooked rice, warm, for serving

Pour the stock into a roomy pot, add the salt and pepper, and bring to a simmer. Add the celery and thyme, cover, and cook for 5 minutes. Add the onion, cover, and cook until the vegetables are completely tender, about 20 minutes. Add the parsley, garlic, and stock powder, cover again, and simmer

Continued on the next page

for a further 5 minutes. Remove from the heat. Taste the soup and adjust the seasonings. Stir through the chicken meat. Cool, cover, and refrigerate overnight.

To serve, reheat the soup. Put a small mound of warm rice in each soup bowl and ladle the soup over. (It's best not to add rice directly to the soup pot unless you're planning to eat it all right away. If it sits too long with rice in it, all the liquid will get absorbed by the starch.)

Salted Caramel Ice Cream

What can I say, the body's cravings are not always virtuous! This recipe comes from a gourmet friend who promised it would be one of the most decadent ice creams I'd ever tasted—and it is! What's peculiar is that the custard is made with whole eggs, rather than just yolks. I don't know if that's the secret, but whatever it is, keep it.

MAKES 4 CUPS/1 LITRE

FOR THE CARAMEL CREAM

1 cup/200 g sugar

1¼ cups/300 ml heavy cream

½ teaspoon vanilla

FOR THE CUSTARD

1 cup/250 ml heavy cream

1 cup/250 ml milk

¼ cup/60 g sugar

3 large eggs

¾ teaspoon Maldon salt

To make the caramel cream, put the sugar in an even layer in a large skillet and set over medium-high heat. Allow to melt and turn to a deep caramel. While this is happening, heat the cream, and when the caramel is ready, whisk in the cream until everything is smooth. Remove from the heat, stir in the vanilla, and set aside to cool.

To make the custard, put the cream and milk in a saucepan with the sugar and bring to a boil. While you wait, crack the eggs into a large bowl and fill the sink with 2 inches of cold water.

When the cream mixture shows its first bubble, gradually whisk it into

Continued on the next page

the eggs, then pour the mixture back into the pot and cook, stirring with a wooden spoon, until the custard leaves a thick, velvety coat on the back. (The test is to draw your finger through it on the back of the spoon. The clear trail should stay put.) This will take only a few minutes. Do not add the salt.

Immediately, strain the custard back into the bowl and stir in the caramel. Set the bowl into the cold water in the sink to cool. Sieve one last time into a clean bowl and refrigerate until very cold, at least 6 hours or overnight.

Before churning, add the salt, then freeze according to your machine's instructions. It will be quite soft when ready, but will firm up further in the freezer.

23

Close to Godliness

A sudden change of season always brings with it a turn of appetite. In the space of a week, we go from craving corn on the cob and to-mato salad to wanting braised beef cheeks in red wine sauce. Time to scrub the grill and put it away for the winter, then to pull for-ward our cast-iron cocottes from the back of the cupboard so they're within easy reach. In spring, of course, it's the other way around: we suddenly turn our noses up at things like squash ravioli and ginger-bread to dive into an orgy of asparagus, strawberries, and peas. We fling open the kitchen windows and let the fresh breezes deliver to our nostrils the hopeful scent of busy earth.

And then our eyes suddenly start lighting upon every cobweb, tea stain, and dust bunny in the house that we somehow managed to overlook all winter. Ugh.

I never plan the day when the urge to purge will be activated, I simply wait for the mood to strike, which I regret to say has not happened this spring as I write these lines. Yes, I notice that the showerhead needs decalcifying and indeed the sunshine has drawn my attention to the state of the windows, but it takes a unique and powerful surge of energy to get me springing from the top of the fridge to inside the toaster oven, and from the cupboard doors to the crisper drawer, not missing an inch with my beady eye and sudsy cloth. (Oh gawd, and it takes hours, too.) I do know that these semi-annual tasks always put me back in touch with every surface and object in my house, reconnecting me to where everything is, what condition it's in, and to what stores we have to use up before their due dates arrive. Cooking is always easier and more pleasant once I'm through, and, strangely, cleaning just the kitchen alone has a way of making the whole house feel purified, not to mention me and my psyche along with it. So why am I dragging my feet?

Funnily enough, though deep cleaning is something I always dread and procrastinate to avoid, routine daily cleaning, like scrubbing the sink and taking out recycling, is something I've got fussier about as I've got older. In the kitchen, especially, this can be irritating for other people. It happens all the time that Peter will get out, say, a mixing bowl and place it on the counter, then wander over to the fridge and come back ready to crack an egg, only to find his bowl mysteriously returned to its spot on the shelf. Or he'll set out a spice to add to a pan of frying onions and, before he has a chance to get so much as a pinch out of the tin, discover it has been nestled back in among the other spice jars by some invisible kitchen gnome. (Ahem.) It's got so that now when he takes something out, he sets it on the counter and barks, "Don't touch that!"

It's not uncommon for people to cook and then clean, in that order. As dinner is prepared, their sinks pile sky-high with dirty dishes, and their countertops turn to rubble heaps of compost—everything from shrimp heads to citrus peelings, oil spills, and eggshells. Amazingly, in that kind of environment, some cooks thrive. Not I. If I am making, say, a salad of grated carrots, the carrot tops and peelings must be off the cutting board and into the compost before any grating begins. If a dusting of flour should land on the floor while I'm baking biscuits, I have to grab a cloth and wipe it away before I even think of reaching for the baking powder. It's not that I'm a clean freak (truly!), but, for me, cooking and cleaning go hand in hand. In fact, part of cooking is cleaning. We have to wash lettuce before we eat it, we trim excess fat off meats before they're cooked, we rinse rice . . . Now that I think of it, nothing was more vehemently drummed into us at cooking school than the need to keep a clean and tidy work station. Otherwise, it's too easy to pick up a rumpled towel and have a knife unexpectedly dive out of it and straight into your foot. Or you can turn a perfectly good piece of cheese into a murder weapon by leaving it for too long on an unwashed spot where a raw chicken thigh was previously sitting. A bit of fanaticism sometimes pays off, which perhaps explains why so many cultures and religions have always been keen on promoting the importance of keeping spic and span.

The famous phrase that links cleanliness to God is attributed to a sermon given in 1778 by the oft-quoted Anglican theologian John Wesley. "Slovenliness is no part of religion," he proclaimed, " . . . cleanliness is indeed next to godliness." I'm not sure what he meant exactly, but presumably that to be clean of spirit, one had also to be clean of body, and to surround oneself with people, places, and things that were likewise pristine. (Good thing he can't see the inside of my fridge!) He's not alone in warning that dirt and clutter attract negativity. I've heard that in India children are told to make their bed, otherwise "the devil will dance upon it." And, in the Chinese tradition of feng shui, any sign of mess is considered a menace to well-being, especially in the kitchen, because it's a room associated with prosperity and health. A dirty stove, according to this school of thought, can have a disastrous effect on career, wealth, and resources; leaking taps can cause your money to go down the drain; even chipped dishes are considered bad luck. So, that does it. I said I needed a surge of energy before I could get motivated to start scrubbing the kitchen. Wrong. All I needed, actually, was a good theological threat and a little superstition.

Beef Consommé with Mushrooms and Madeira

Few foods are cleaner or more restorative than this. You can, of course, cut this recipe short by buying tinned consommé and just adding the mushrooms and Madeira, but there's something therapeutic about seeing cloudy brown stock turn to clear, sparkling broth by your own hand, a process known as clarifying. Besides, your own homemade stock or good stock from a butcher will taste better and give you better control over the salt. (Note that this recipe will not work with stock sold in Tetra Paks.) One warning: if you've never seen a "raft"—the mixture added to the broth that will form a thick foam all over top to trap impurities—be warned, it's ugly. Don't worry, though, because it gets removed once its job is done.

SERVES 4

TO CLARIFY THE STOCK TO CONSOMMÉ

8 cups/2 litres brown stock, homemade or from the butcher, cold
4 ounces/110 g lean ground beef
1 small carrot, thinly sliced
1 small onion or leek, sliced
¼ celery rib, cut into pieces
A handful of fresh flat-leaf parsley leaves
A handful of fresh thyme leaves
4 egg whites
Salt and pepper

FOR SERVING

2 cups very thinly sliced raw mushrooms (about 5 ounces/150 g)
2 tablespoons Madeira, or to taste

Continued on the next page

To make the consommé, put the stock in a roomy pot. Mince the beef, carrot, onion, celery, parsley, and thyme together in a food processor. Whisk the egg whites to frothy, then whisk in the meat mixture, and finally whisk it all into the stock. Place over medium-high heat, and bring to a boil, stirring occasionally to prevent sticking to the bottom of the pot, until a thick froth forms on the surface. Stop stirring, reduce the heat, make an opening in the raft in the centre or to the side of the pot, and simmer gently for 30 minutes.

Without disturbing the raft, gently ladle the consommé through the opening to a cheesecloth-lined sieve set over a bowl. Allow it to drip through without forcing. The resulting liquid should be perfectly clear. Taste, and season with salt and pepper. Discard the raft. If you're not going to eat the consommé right away, transfer it to a container and refrigerate until serving time.

To serve, put the mushrooms in a pot and add 2 cups of the consommé. Bring to a boil and simmer for 3 minutes. Add the remaining consommé and heat through, then stir in the Madeira before ladling into hot bowls.

Prosperity Salad

Every Lunar New Year, a friend invites us for a celebratory feast which starts with this exciting and delicious salad. All the ingredients are arranged on a platter, then, just before serving, the dressing is poured over and everyone ceremonially thrusts in their chopsticks to toss it as high as they can because the higher the toss, the better the chances of luck in the year ahead. This is surely the healthiest holiday dish I've ever heard of, and it's wonderful to eat because every bite is different. Note that the list of vegetables is not carved in stone. Sometimes people add shredded iceberg lettuce or cellophane noodles, bean sprouts, watermelon radish, Asian peas, julienned red bell pepper . . . You see plenty of variation, so if there's something you can't find, don't sweat it.

SERVES 4 AS A FIRST COURSE

FOR THE DRESSING
3 tablespoons soy sauce
1½ tablespoons rice wine vinegar
2 teaspoons toasted sesame oil
1 teaspoon mirin
1 garlic clove, grated

FOR THE SALAD
4 ounces/110 g sliced sushi-grade salmon, gravlax, or smoked
  salmon
1 pomelo or pink grapefruit, sectioned
½ cup/50 g finely julienned carrot
½ cup/50 g julienned Lebanese cucumber
½ cup/50 g shredded red cabbage
½ cup/50 g julienned snow peas

Continued on the next page

½ cup/50 g pickled turnip or julienned red bell pepper

½ cup/50 g julienned jicama or daikon

3 green onions, thinly sliced on the diagonal

A large handful of fresh coriander leaves

3 tablespoons sesame seeds

FOR GARNISH

Japanese pickled ginger

Roasted, salted peanuts

Deep-fried Asian noodles or sliced wontons

For the dressing, mix the soy sauce, vinegar, sesame oil, mirin, and garlic in a small bowl and set aside.

For the salad, place the salmon at the centre of a large round platter. Arrange heaps of the grapefruit, carrot, cucumber, cabbage, snow peas, pickled turnip, jicama, green onion, and coriander leaves all around it in a ring, then scatter over the sesame seeds. Put the garnishes in separate bowls.

To serve, set the salad and garnishes on the table. Pour the dressing over the salad, then invite everyone to join in the ceremony of tossing with chopsticks, and serving themselves.

24

Nothing Heroic

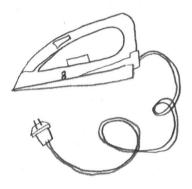

Out for a stroll one day, waiting for a red light to change, I caught an ear-pricking exchange between a father and his daughter. Judging by her height and her Barbie-pink backpack, the little girl must have been about seven. "No," her father was saying to her, "brushing your hair is not a chore and brushing your teeth is not a chore. It's household jobs that are chores: taking out the garbage, washing the dishes, making your bed . . . " The little girl was listening with narrowed eyes, her mind in limbo between suspicion and potential enlightenment. The light turned green, and that's the full extent of the story I got, but for some reason that snippet of familial education did laps in my brain for the rest of my walk.

I can see how it would be hard for a child to draw a line between what's supposed to be a chore and what's a privilege. When we're little, we just want to do what we see big people doing, so if that's washing the car, then we're right in there with a little rag of our own rubbing away at a hubcap as happy as clams. I hold a fine scene in my memory of one of my brothers a few years ago: he's lying on his back under the kitchen sink with a wrench, while his two-year-old sits alongside wielding a screwdriver, merrily pretending to be repairing the cupboard door while her father deals with the leaking pipe and represses urges to get colourful with the English language. Moral of the story: just as one man's trash is another man's treasure, one man's chore is another man's leisure.

When I got home, I looked it up. Chore is a variant of char (as in charwoman) and it comes from the Middle English "cherre" ("odd job"). Today, it refers to a routine task, generally of the domestic sort, and as a secondary meaning it can also refer to a task that is unpleasant, but necessary, the kind of work that, if we could possibly farm it out to somebody else, we would in a heartbeat: mopping floors, ironing, cleaning windows . . . just as the little girl's father had been explaining. But part of me questions the negative spin on these activities. Over the past few years, I've had a change of heart when it comes to domestic duties (more on which in a bit), and in light of that, I wondered how I might have responded to the little girl if she'd asked me.

Cooking, I suppose, would get lumped into the category of chores by a certain number of people. I have some friends who can't stand it. Luckily for me, with rare exceptions, I have always found cooking to be a pacifier and a joy. On those empty weekend afternoons, just back from a market with a bulging basket, there's nothing more pleasant than puttering around the kitchen turning cherries into a juicy, shirt-staining tart. Or in winter, what better way to warm the soul than by spending the day hovering over a stew, then pouring a fat glass of wine afterwards to sip at slowly while watching the snow fall outside? But I suppose that's when we have time and an appetite, and are in the right frame of mind. It can't be denied that moments do arise when the prospect of having to produce a meal for people does hang over us like a cloud of doom, and we must find ways to turn the dreaded chore with our name on it into something more energizing and fulfilling than it is draining.

In my most desperate moments, I pull out a pair of words that I've always used when I'm not in the mood for exercise: "nothing heroic." When I'm feeling about as keen to go for a run as, say, one might be to visit the proctologist, these words are a useful reminder that I don't have to go out and try to be the next Usain Bolt, I just have to go trot around for a while and that's enough. I guess the moral of that story is that when there's something you don't want to do, begin, and soon it will be behind you. Interestingly, once I'm out on the street and into my rhythm, I always feel fine, and often even run longer and better than expected. The culinary equivalent would be telling myself that all I have to do is make an omelet. Worst-case scenario: people get a slender, rolled-up egg dish with a glass of wine and are then sent on their merry way. Better case, if beating the eggs gets me to my second wind, people may find themselves sitting down to a frittata containing chèvre and greens, a tomato salad, and perhaps even the aforementioned cherry tart to end.

Another tactic I use in times when culinary motivation is absent is to go into the fridge in the morning and root out one or two things that need to be eaten, set them on the counter, and wait. As the day goes on, I can almost feel the cauliflower and heel of Gruyère follow me around with their eyes. I don't actively think about what to do with them, but I am aware of their presence, and somehow that awareness works away on my subconscious mind until it eventually decides to produce an evening meal of, say, Swiss fondue with roasted cauliflower for dipping. That actually happened one night and I thought it was rather brilliant.

Today there's a bunch of yellow beets and half a cantaloupe on the counter. I'm hoping by mid-afternoon they'll have got in touch with that far-off region of my brain responsible for coming up with supper and given it a few hints. If they don't, then I'll swap them for some other option—there's a fennel bulb in the fridge and some ground turkey—and see if that works. As a general rule, having tasks put right in front of us tends to lead to their getting done. Try setting a basket of ironing in the middle of the dining room table rather than leaving it in the laundry room and you'll see what I mean.

I was saying that the way I approach household chores has changed of late. I can't tell you what triggered it, but it has been quite revolutionary. Instead of feeling like a slave to dirty dishes or rumpled laundry, I've started to see myself as a sort of healer going about shifting the energy of things from negative to positive. The frying pan with bits of rice sticking to its side, with my loving touch suddenly gleams from its hook like a decorated soldier on parade. The linen shirt which, minutes before, looked like a crumpled wad of paper destined for the bin, now falls from its hanger with perfect posture, as smooth and elegant as a holy robe. It makes me feel strangely powerful to be able to transform things in this way. Even the most minor action—tossing a deceased bouquet of ranunculus, or straightening a pile of magazines on the coffee table—has an immediate, palpable, positive impact. To do chores is to plod through life like a donkey; to make light out of darkness is divine. You see, there's more depth and possibility to the term "domestic goddess" than we give it credit for.

Discomfort motivates. If our hands are sticky, we wash them. If our tooth aches, we take it to the dentist. If the banana in the fruit bowl is in its final days, we eat it or pop it into the freezer for later baking. I've just put the melon and beets away and taken two fillets of sole from the freezer. Once they've thawed, I'll set them on the counter, and seeing them there, limp and wet, will trigger my brain into urgently wanting to take care of them. "Flour me and fry me in butter," the fish will say. "Serve me with lemon and some baby broccoli. Nothing heroic." And, despite my lack of enthusiasm for cooking tonight, I will oblige and come out the victor, saviour of the sole and master of the chore, not its minion.

Sole with Capers and Blackened Lemon

Tasty, elegant, and ready in a few effortless minutes, this is a save-the-day sort of dish. Serve with baby broccoli and/or buttered baby potatoes.

SERVES 2

1 small lemon, halved

½ cup/60 g flour (gluten-free is fine), for dredging

Salt and pepper

2 tablespoons clarified butter

2 thick fillets of sole, about 5 ounces/140 g each

1 tablespoon butter

1 tablespoon capers, rinsed and barely chopped

1 tablespoon finely chopped fresh flat-leaf parsley leaves

Heat a small cast-iron pan on high. Lay in the lemon halves, cut side down, and leave until the bases blacken, 3 to 4 minutes. Set aside.

Heavily season the flour with salt and pepper. Heat the clarified butter in a skillet until hot and foaming. Dip the fish into the flour to coat, then lay straight in the sizzling butter and fry until cooked through and golden, about 3 minutes per side. Remove the fish to a serving plate.

Add the regular butter to the pan and allow it to brown slightly. Toss in the capers for a few seconds, then the parsley. Pour over the fish, and add the blackened lemon to the platter for squeezing. Serve immediately.

A Simple Cherry Tart

The perfection of this as a dessert cannot be overstated. Serve it plain.

MAKES ONE 7-INCH/18-CM TART

FOR THE PERFECT PASTRY

1 cup/125 g flour

¼ cup/60 g salted butter, softened

¼ cup/30 g icing sugar

2 tablespoons almond flour

1 egg yolk

2 tablespoons cold water

FOR THE FILLING

1 pound/450 g cherries

½ cup/100 ml sugar

2 tablespoons cornstarch

¾ cup/175 ml water

For the pastry, put the flour, butter, icing sugar, and almond flour in a food processor and whizz to crumbs. Add the egg yolk and water and pulse just until it comes together. Do not overmix. Spill onto a work surface and pat into a disk. Wrap in plastic and refrigerate for 2 hours.

Roll out the pastry between 2 layers of plastic wrap, fit it into a 7-inch/ 18-cm tart pan, then refrigerate while you prepare the filling. Heat the oven to 350°F/180°C.

For the filling, first pit the cherries, then put them in a saucepan with the sugar. Dissolve the cornstarch in a little of the water, slurry style, then mix in the rest of the water and pour over the cherries. Bring to a boil, giving the mixture a stir, then reduce to a simmer and cook for 10 minutes.

Continued on the next page

Remove the pastry from the fridge, pour in the filling, and bake the tart for 45 minutes. Remove to a rack to cool before transferring to a serving platter.

Brandied Cherries

If the tart, however simple, does feel too heroic, this is a nice alternative. Pull the stems off 1 pound/450 g cherries, but leave the pits in. Place them in a saucepan and add ½ cup/100 g sugar and the juice of a lemon. Just before you're ready to eat dessert, bring to a boil and simmer for 10 minutes. Remove the cherries to a serving bowl with a slotted spoon, then boil the juices for a few minutes to reduce somewhat. Stir in a tablespoon of brandy, then pour the sauce over the cherries. Serve immediately with vanilla ice cream. Warn people of the pits!

25

The Trusty Gut

"Well, I've just ruined a perfectly good squash," my mother said down the phone. It seemed unlikely, but when she explained that she'd allowed herself to be lured by a dubious internet recipe for squash soup, I understood. "They always want you to add all kinds of things that have no business being in the recipe," she complained. "Celery, carrot, potato, paprika . . . I should just have done it my way." Oh, how I know only too well that feeling when you're reading a recipe and your instincts stand on end, but you ignore the warnings because some part of your brain has told you to bow down to the supposed authority of the printed word.

I had a similar experience last week. I had been alerted to a recipe for whole candied oranges, which sounded like just my kind of dessert. The cookbook in which I tracked it down included a promising picture, but I found my lips pursing into a skeptical "hmm" when I read that four oranges were going to be candied in a single cup of sugar syrup. The recipe even had the gall to stress that, to achieve even translucence, the oranges should be regularly rotated and dunked below the surface of this mirror of syrup, and not just left to float. Picture four basketballs in a mud puddle and see just how likely any dunking would be to occur. Another questionable instruction was to put stripes all around the oranges at half-inch intervals for decoration, using a channeling tool, but to make sure the fruit didn't split during the initial poaching in water. Every one of my oranges split . . . right along all those helpful fault lines I'd just created. I decided to plough on with the candying process, despite the fact that the fruit now looked as though it had been through a serious ordeal (as had I!). For safety, I doubled the amount of syrup, but it still came only about halfway up the oranges. After twice the length of recommended poaching time, during which I constantly turned them over, the fruit emerged only faintly candied in patches. So, it was destination compost for my four navel oranges, procured at a resentful $1.60 apiece. My self-confidence went into the bin with them.

I always kick myself when I know better but nonetheless set judgement aside in favour of listening to someone who I assume must know better than me, even though they're a total stranger. At least, whenever I experience such a thing, it brings me back to my senses. Some recipes are more reliable than others, everybody knows that; but no recipe—not even the ones we've made dozens of times before—is gospel. The quality of our ingredients, the weather, our mood, the sharpness of our knives, the heaviness of our pan . . . no end of things can affect how a dish works out, which is why the process of cooking always needs our full involvement, why we must stay in communication with every recipe from beginning to end. "The goal is to go from being subordinate to recipes to being their equal," as Peter put it one day.

For a long time, I was a slave to the much-touted vinaigrette rule: three to one, as in three parts oil to one part vinegar. For whatever reason, I never felt I could diverge from the formula, though it never seemed to taste quite right, so I'd start with that and try adding other ingredients, constantly coming up with unsatisfactory vinaigrettes. It got so I hated making them at all. If I was preparing greens before a meal and anyone politely happened to offer, "Is there anything I can do?"—probably thinking I might ask them to fill water glasses or call people to the table—boom! they'd immediately be put on vinaigrette duty. I'd do anything to get off the hook and not risk the humiliation of producing something either throat-arrestingly acidic or unctuously blah. Who'd have thought those few seemingly innocent ingredients—oil, vinegar, and salt—could be so intimidating?

There are many bonuses to reaching middle age, and finally being able to trust myself with salad dressing is one of them, along with feeling fine about going to bed before ten and not having one sweet clue who the faces belong to on the cover of *Hello!* magazine. I don't remember when it was that I finally got the hang of what are essentially salad sauces, but it certainly had to do with abandoning that carved-in-stone formula and experimenting with a wider scale. Now, I know that when I want a sharp, palate-cleansing dressing, say for a leafy salad to follow a beef stew, I use Peter's ratio: 5 tablespoons of olive oil to 3 tablespoons of red wine vinegar, along with a grated garlic clove, salt, and pepper. Most of the time, I use less acid than that, especially where Dijon mustard is involved, though my mother has an excellent recipe for dressing that contains equal amounts of oil and vinegar, along with Dijon, soy, and a pinch of sugar. The point is that you can only make a good dressing once you've acquired enough experience and self-esteem to trust your own tongue.

Another area in which I've learned to listen more carefully to myself is where superfluous ingredients are asked for in recipes. I found a good carrot salad recipe not long ago, which sounded interesting because it was garnished with fried shallot. The first time I made it, the shallots were too heavy and oily because the instructions were to fry them in a little oil "until crisp," which of course never happened. To get them crisp, they needed a lot of oil so they'd deep-fry, which I did the second time, only to realize that the little squiggles, even that way, weighed everything down and distracted too much from the otherwise fresh, light, lime-dressed carrot. I got rid of the shallots, along with a couple of other ingredients, until I finally had a salad that felt right to me. This underscored the fact that, ultimately, the only real version of any recipe is our own.

Mind you, sometimes even our own recipes can't be trusted. I once turned to a recipe in a cookbook that I had written, only to discover an entire paragraph missing from the method. What can I say? Mistakes happen. I am consoled, at least, to know I'm not the only one with clay feet. Even my exacting teacher from long ago, Anne Willan, has what can only be called an adorable typo in one of her books. The yield in a recipe for "meringue swans" clearly went back and forth so many times between saying how many swans the recipe made to how many people the recipe served that by the time it went to print, it read, "Serves 12 swans."

"You've gotta use your head, see," my late grandfather was fond of saying. I don't know why it's so easy to shut down whenever we're handed a list of instructions: laziness perhaps, or self-protection against failure—though, to hand the reins of power to someone else, no matter what the situation, is never guaranteed to save us from defeat. It merely gives us someone else to blame when it happens. Well, what good does that do? All things considered, if we're going to choose a situation in which to see what happens when we ignore our intuition, then trying a new and potentially dubious recipe is relatively safe. Let it fail. Let us be reminded we should have known better. And then, maybe let's even try again, this time listening to our sagacious inner voices, and see what happens. On that note, I should probably swallow my pride and go take another stab at those pesky oranges, but I'm all tuned in to my gut now, you see, and I'm afraid it's saying, "Nah."

Mum's Salad Dressing

Balsamic vinegar is no longer in vogue, as it once was, but my mother couldn't care less. She uses it in this rather mysterious combination of ingredients to make a light salad dressing with serious taste and depth. Whenever I serve it on salad, people always lift their heads and remark, "Nice dressing!"

MAKES ABOUT ½ CUP/125 ML

¼ teaspoon Dijon mustard
½ teaspoon soy sauce
½ teaspoon sugar
1 garlic clove, grated
¼ cup/60 ml balsamic vinegar
¼ cup/60 ml grapeseed or avocado oil
Salt and pepper

Whisk together the Dijon, soy sauce, sugar, and garlic, then whisk in the vinegar, and finally the oil. Alternatively, put all the ingredients in a jar, secure the lid, and shake like mad. Taste, and adjust the seasonings.

Asian Carrot Salad

Fresh and addictive, this is my favourite carrot salad.

SERVES 4

4 carrots (14 ounces/390 g), grated
2 tablespoons lime juice
1 tablespoon Thai fish sauce
1 Thai red chili pepper, seeded and minced
½ teaspoon sugar
½ teaspoon salt
Two handfuls of roughly chopped fresh coriander leaves
A handful of fresh mint leaves, torn
¼ cup/40 g roasted, salted peanuts, roughly chopped

Put the carrots in a bowl. Whisk together the lime juice, fish sauce, chili pepper, sugar, and salt, then toss with the carrots. Add the coriander, mint, and peanuts, and toss to distribute evenly. Taste and adjust the seasonings, then transfer to a serving dish.

26

The Final Feast

The evening with friends ended on the death-row dinner question: What would you want to eat for your last meal on earth? I've never quite understood why anyone would want to contemplate such a thing because, honestly, if you knew you were about to croak, would you really have an appetite? Our party had somehow led itself around to this curious question via a discussion about most memorable meals of our lives. Someone remembered one in Brazil, another in central France, another in Milan, and the funny thing in every case was that nobody remembered the actual food, but rather the place, the occasion, the ambiance, a detail, or the people they had been with. In Brazil, it had been the font on the restaurant sign that stood out foremost in our friend Paul's mind. ("So bad it was awesome.") In central France (my memory), it was the fact that a man at a neighbouring table was sharing his meal with an Afghan hound: one forkful for monsieur, one forkful for Fido. Same fork. Gross. Then there was that meal two autumns ago, the one in the garden that we'd all attended . . . Sinclair had brought fresh sardines, but what had come after that? Nobody had a clue. All we could remember were the autumn leaves and the general debauchery.

When you think of how significant meals seem in the moment—not to mention how much effort we put into creating them—it's remarkable how forgettable virtually all of them end up being. When I try to recall the best of my life, I can never dredge up more than a handful, and, even then, the memories are only ever of very specific moments. One "best" would be a lunch in a garden restaurant in the Camargue, in southern France not far from Arles. It went on for a full afternoon, but my mind has condensed it to the sound of gravel crunching underfoot as the waiters came and went from our table, and to the moment our first course landed before us: sardines (again), this time on a small, smoking grill. Another outstanding meal in my brain's souvenir box took place in Assisi with my parents, but it too has now been reduced to nothing but the slightly claustrophobic sensation of being under stone arches and the fact that my mother ordered a zucchini-flower soup that sent her into raptures. I once went fishing on Vancouver Island with friends and, afterwards, we built a fire in a place called Dead Man's Cove for a picnic. Presumably there was fish, but what I've ended up remembering, instead of anything wiggling on a hook then finding itself in a frying pan, is trawling the beach with my friend Clara in search of driftwood that would make "Martha-worthy plates." That, and unwrapping fruitcake for everyone to have a crumbling slice of with a warming shot of whisky after lunch.

But perhaps it's those moments that meals are made of anyway. They are intended to be "lived in the now," experienced like a dance or a concert, not kept in frames or on shelves, though I suppose printed menus could be. All I remember about the movie version of

Cyrano de Bergerac is the word "panache" at the very end. Something about how the "p" was pronounced has always stuck, because it was uttered with the kind of force you'd put into blowing out a candle. Same sort of useless, but poetic, little memory that the brain keeps in its pocket like a magic stone for rubbing between the fingers when it needs pacifying.

I guess this explains why delicious individual dishes are more likely to stand out than whole meals, too. A few weeks ago, my friend Tammy made a salad out of white radicchio and frisée, bejeweled with toasted pumpkin seeds, sunflower seeds, and sesame seeds as well as some thinly sliced buttery cheese, all dressed with bacon fat, grapeseed oil, and pear vinegar from Normandy. It was so exquisite it has blotted out the rest of the meal. I had brown rice cooked in ham stock once that I'd love to have again. Still clear in my mind's eye, and on my mind's tongue, is a long-ago orange-flower-water ice cream sliding across the surface of a crêpe Suzette. And there was that crisp-skinned chicken with a star-anise glaze on carrots that someone called Casper made once in Paris. I could never replicate it, no matter how many times I tried.

And yet, when it came around to my turn to respond to the dreaded question of what to feast on before being made to walk the plank, none of those most-memorable dishes even crossed my mind as worthy menu items. Peter said he'd ask for steak frites. Paul declared the Québécois version of a full English breakfast as his ultimate off-to-meet-my-maker meal (see page 205). Horia wanted polenta, Luiza porcini mushrooms. Jane is the only one who thought she'd want a three-star meal, but she gave no specifics. I found myself saying, "A baked potato from my father's garden, and then a final cup of tea."

There is no bottom to the barrel of mindfulness tricks meant to help bring us back to the present moment and ferret out the true state of our own minds when they seem too foggy to penetrate. One of them is to ask, "What am I doing right now and why am I doing it?" Sample answer: "I'm twirling my fingers in my hair because . . . I'm anxious . . . because . . . I have to give a speech . . ." Or, "I'm vacuuming the living room because I don't want to sit down at my desk . . . because . . . that person on Zoom makes me nervous . . . because . . ." I tried this out on my response to the death-row question to try to get at the reasoning behind it. "I'd want a baked potato from my father's garden because . . . because it would be from the same earth I grew up on (and which I am no doubt half full of) and it would connect me to my father. I would want a cup of tea because . . . because growing up, my mother was rarely without a teacup in her hand. You'd find them, saucer-less, left absent-mindedly all over the house. The tea would connect me to my mother, and then it would be fine for me to go.

Instinctively, it feels distasteful to speak about food and death in the same breath, which may explain why I've always recoiled at the last-meal-on-Earth question. In any case, when the time draws near for me to drift over to the other side, my only concern will be about getting the cellar stocked with bottles of Champagne, loading the freezer with casseroles, and setting up assembly lines for making funeral sandwiches and sickeningly sweet squares. Then, I'll float up to heaven on an empty stomach, light as a party balloon, and blissfully enjoy the view of my final feast being devoured.

Corpse Reviver #2

Peter and I have a pre-dinner-party ritual we call "a psychological," which is a quiet cocktail the two of us share before any guests show up. This one is my favourite: a refreshing, lemony drink, which includes the aromatized wine-based aperitif called Lillet along with a judicious splash of absinthe for a hint of anise. True to its name, it's a booster of body and mood both. I intend to arrange for buckets of it to be served at my funeral.

MAKES 1 COCKTAIL

1 ounce gin
1 ounce orange liqueur
1 ounce Lillet or Cocchi Americano
1 ounce lemon juice
Vague splash of absinthe (about ⅛ teaspoon)

Fill a shaker with ice; add the gin, orange liqueur, Lillet, lemon juice, and absinthe; cover; and shake vigorously, before straining into a chilled glass.

A Perfect Baked Potato

Every August when I visit my parents, my father's garden is at its peak, and while all the vegetables are glorious, it's the potatoes that are his pride and joy. He slaves over the plants for months, spreading worm poop around their bases for fertilizer and heading out every morning to kill potato bugs by hand, "before they turn into fornicating teenagers." By the time they're ready to harvest, the potatoes are a true delicacy: rare, earthy wonders of buttery tenderness, their baked skins not leathery, but crackling crisp as your fork shatters through. This baking method that I came across in *Cook's Illustrated* is the best I've ever found.

SERVES 1

1 organic baking potato
Salt
Olive oil, for rubbing
Butter, for serving
Pepper

Heat the oven to 450°F/230°C. Set a baking sheet in the oven beneath the rack where the potato will go.

Poke the potato on both ends and on all sides with a fork or metal skewer. Scrub the potato clean, then salt it all over while still wet, and set on the rack in the oven above the baking sheet. Bake until tender, 60 to 70 minutes. Remove from the oven, rub all over with oil, then put back in for a further 10 minutes to crispen.

Remove the potato from the oven and transfer to a plate. Slash an X into the top, and give the potato a squeeze so it opens up slightly. Put in some butter, salt, and pepper, and mix in with a fork, fluffing the potato flesh as you do so. Savour like it's your last meal on earth.

Fried Potato Skins

I've already told you about this, but in case you need reminding, these are always a serious treat. Eat your potato flesh only, saving the skin, which you then cut into chip-sized pieces and fry in butter until crisp. Salt, eat for "dessert," die, and go to heaven.

27

Considering Breakfast

For what you'd think would be the easiest meal of the day, breakfast sure is a tricky topic. It's the most personal meal, taken at arguably the most vulnerable and private time of the day, and so I suppose it's understandable that people should be set in their ways when it comes to how they want it. What a minefield for a host, though!

Friends of the introverted persuasion were recently moaning about having stayed with people who, with all the best intentions I'm sure, had foisted upon them a huge and elaborate breakfast when all they desperately wanted was the company of a cup of coffee and a newspaper. Out came the smoked salmon, the waffles, the grapes and watermelon, the freshly baked homemade Danishes, some eggy casserole number . . . You have no choice in a situation like that but to eat and do your best to be chipper, but it can be torture when you're not in the mood.

I sympathized because even on the best of days I'm a similar morning type to them, which is to say antisocial and unhungry. My idea of a perfect start to the day is tea and peace, preferably alone or with just my other half, who is only ever there in body at that hour anyway because his mental focus is entirely on the crosswords. I consider this a lucky aspect of our marriage. Woe would be me if I had to wake up every day to the smell of bacon and the sound of a radio blaring out international bad news. Instead, I can step over the threshold from breakfast to the rest of the day quietly reading my mail, sorting out my "to do" lists, and checking the diary. If I am robbed of this sacred moment (about two hours' worth of sacred moments, if I'm honest), then I start off scattered and anxious, and with a frown line so deep it looks like an earthquake has opened a fissure in my brow. Apparently, I'm as stubborn when it comes to breakfast as the next guy.

I remember hosting an American visitor in Paris once and being rather annoyed because he turned the entire first day of his trip into a scavenger hunt to find oatmeal. Maybe with the healthy food movements, and more multiculturalism, it's easier to find there these days, but back then oatmeal was simply not readily available on Parisian grocery shelves. High and low we searched, dragging ourselves from one arrondissement to the next, ignoring every garden, every museum, every café, every splendid view, until, at last, at about the aperitif hour, we finally found a bag of oatmeal in a health-food store somewhere near Bastille that would promise him his all-important bowl of porridge the following morning. No when-in-Rome razzmatazz for that guy!

Perhaps it was that incident that prompted me to start asking overnight guests "What do you eat for breakfast?" right up front, just like you ask dinner guests if they have any food allergies the moment you invite them. That way, you don't get an urgent need for almond milk sprung on you at the crack of dawn when all you ever have in the fridge is table cream. As long as you've stocked guests' habitual morning supplies (the beauty of breakfast is that, for the most part, people like to eat the same thing every day), the meal should be a relative breeze to produce, especially if you do what I do, which is lay things out the night before, or at least make them easy to find, and tell people to help themselves. Lazy? Perhaps, but if I've got people staying with me, whom presumably I've wined and dined the night before, then I really don't want to exhaust myself and mess up the kitchen all over again first thing by making blueberry pancakes for one guest, and fruit salad with yoghurt and granola for another, and toad in the hole for another, like some kind of harried line cook.

Perhaps if I had a breakfast room, like the ones you find in rambling country houses, I'd adopt a different attitude. I was just reading *Etiquette of Good Society* (1893), by one Lady Colin Campbell (not the present-day incarnation, which is too bad, because I'd breakfast with her any day), wherein she describes such a room so enchantingly it nearly gave me a craving for a kipper. "And then in summer to enter a sunny, cheerful room," she writes, "(a breakfast-room should, if possible, be so situated as to catch the early rays of the sun), with its wide-open window, through which enters the cool, fresh morning air, the scent of flowers and the song of the birds; the table prettily decked with buds and blossoms; luscious tempting fruit lying perdu in nests of green leaves; crisp rolls and golden butter . . . " A dream!

One nice thing about a breakfast room like that is that people are welcome to drift in and out at their leisure, what with there being no firmly set eating hour nor any single meal served. Instead, it's a buffet on a sideboard from which people help themselves. First coffee or tea, then if you want a boiled egg and toast, you have that; if you'd rather Froot Loops, there's the box, and so on. Another nice thing is that as long as there are enough people coming and going, it loosens the rules around any need to socialize, so morning-averse people can be their grouchy selves without offending anyone. One can stare out the window daydreaming and munching on toast while another books a plane ticket, phone in one hand and coffee in the other, and another reads the paper, only occasionally looking up to share a remark—"Can you believe the weather in Rangoon?" or "Looks like the old post office is being turned into another cannabis store."—before bowing their head down again in absorbed silence. Right out of Evelyn Waugh. (Note to self: Don't pray for a breakfast room without simultaneously praying for servants.)

There is actually a way to have your cake and eat it too, as I discovered once when we overnighted with friends in the Laurentians who live on a quiet, pristine lake. Having feasted royally the night before and slept like a felled oak, I got up extra early, swam, did yoga, showered, and got in my two hours' peace before anyone else roused. By the time the rest of the gang showed up and the coffee machine was fired up, I had actually worked up the appetite of a farmhand, so when it was announced we'd all be sitting down to "the full Québécois," I found myself uncharacteristically ecstatic at the prospect.

Such a breakfast is a wonderful thing to behold as it's being made, for a start. The sizzle of bacon, the scent of toasting bagels, the sweetness of warming maple-flavoured beans, the crisp, bubbling edges of eggs frying in butter . . . every element is truly a feast for all five senses. And when it's ready, one shared meal for everyone, it can only be treated in a dinnerly way, which it was. We sat at the table together and feasted forth, not each in our own bubble of brain fog, but truly together, talking about everything under the sun from the significance of geometric shapes to the pleasures of Paris, to all the stupid mistakes we've ever made in our lives. You don't get that kind of conversation and connection over a smoothie, even if it is at the most intimate hour of the day. So, there's something to be said about shedding our steel-cut morning habits and, once in a while at least, trying something new.

The Full Québécois
(à la Paul Lavoie)

It's maple baked beans, Montreal bagels, and the French-Canadian pork pâté known as cretons that distinguish this hearty breakfast from its English counterpart.

SERVES 4

1 15-ounce/425-g tin maple beans

4 slices ripe summer tomato

8 to 12 slices bacon

4 to 8 eggs

2 bagels, halved for toasting

Butter for the bagels

4 pinches of fresh sprouts

A pot of cretons or rillettes, for serving

Heat the beans in a small pot. Meanwhile, lay a slice of tomato on each of 4 dinner plates. Fry the bacon, and remove to paper towel to drain. Fry the eggs in the fat of the bacon left behind in the pan. Toast the bagels, and butter them.

Arrange the bacon on the plates next to the tomato. Cut the bagel halves in half and set 2 pieces on each plate. Slide on an egg, and scatter with sprouts. Finally, put a good spoonful of warm beans into each of 4 small serving dishes, and set one on each plate. Serve, letting people help themselves to the cretons to spread on their bagels.

Date and Squash Loaf

This is a most delicious, moist loaf, perfect with a cup of tea, whether at breakfast or in the afternoon. Die-hards butter their slices, of course.

MAKES ONE 9 × 5-INCH/23 × 12-CM LOAF

½ cup/110 g butter, softened

1½ cups/300 g sugar

2 eggs, lightly beaten

1 cup/250 g cooked, puréed squash (or leftover pumpkin from making a pie)

1 tablespoon grated orange rind

¼ cup/60 ml orange juice

2¼ cups/280 g flour

½ teaspoon baking powder

2 teaspoons baking soda

½ teaspoon salt

½ teaspoon ground cinnamon

½ teaspoon ground cloves

½ cup/80 g chopped Medjool dates (5 or 6 dates, pitted)

Heat the oven to 350°F/180°C. Line the base of a 9 × 5-inch/23 × 12-cm loaf pan with parchment.

Cream together the butter and sugar, then beat in the eggs. Stir through the squash, orange rind, and orange juice. Sift the flour, baking powder, baking soda, salt, cinnamon, and cloves into a medium bowl and toss the chopped dates in, working with your hands to keep the pieces separate. Stir the date mixture into the squash mixture to combine thoroughly, and pour into the loaf pan.

Bake until a toothpick inserted in the centre comes out clean, about an hour. Remove from the oven and let sit for 5 minutes. Go around the edges of the pan with a knife, and invert onto a cooling rack to cool completely.

28

A Place at the Table

When I was studying in Munich in my early twenties, I had a Scottish friend called Gina who came from somewhere outside Glasgow. Gina was living with a family in a grand house in Bogenhausen, and I was across the river in another swish quarter called Schwabing. On our days off, Gina and I would meet up somewhere in the middle and roam the city in search of the best pastry shops, or we'd go sit in the Englischer Garten with pretzels and pilsners and compare notes. Whenever she'd tasted something that knocked her socks off, she'd bring me the recipe. I still have one for "Gina's Schokoladen Küchen" and another for chicken in cream sauce with toasted almonds. Gina had an appetite for things rich.

When the holidays came around, Gina invited me to join her at her family home, and a few days after she left, I made my own way to the United Kingdom and up to her far end of it. Trains and coaches were presumably involved, and several of them, too, because by the time I reached the remote destination she called home, somewhere in Ayrshire, if memory serves, I felt as though I'd travelled to another planet altogether. After the relative grandeur of Munich, Gina's little town was grey, grim, and empty, with only a few practical shops along the high street—a butcher, a chemist, a grocer. Beyond that, across a bridge, stretched row upon row of council houses, one of which turned out to be where Gina's family lived.

I'd never been anywhere like this in my life. It was strange to see Gina at home in a context so different from the one I'd come to know her in, namely a giant white mansion with a ten-foot dining table and silver cutlery so heavy it felt like lifting barbells. She'd seemed completely at home with that, too, but I could see it must have taken some time. Here in Scotland, under a tin-coloured sky, the house of her childhood was reminiscent of a block of cement. You entered it through a narrow door, I seem to recall, and were immediately greeted by a steep, narrow staircase covered in pink shag carpet that led up to a couple of bedrooms. On the main floor, I remember only two rooms to poke a nose into: a kitchen and a living room, both low-lit. In the kitchen, there was a sort of flap against the wall near the door that you could prop up as a make-shift bar to eat at, although nobody ever bothered. The living room consisted of a sofa facing a television set, with a coffee table in between, and that's where the family ate. That was the first time I'd ever set foot in a house that didn't have a dining table, and my astonishment at the time cannot be exaggerated.

We all grow up with assumptions about what the world is like beyond the narrow slivers of it we actually know, and clearly one of mine was that every house had at least one dining table. Where I grew up, that most reassuring of pieces of furniture was at the heart of practically everything we did, eaten at three times a day and, between meals, covered with paper: drawings, newspapers, homework, letters, bills, projects. Not only did I take our table for granted, but also the fact that I belonged at it, that there would always be a place for me there, and that whenever I came to it, it would restore me. I've been around long enough now to realize what a privilege it has been to live a life in which the right to a place at a table has always been assumed normal. For someone like Gina, although she certainly had a warm and welcoming place within her family, that privilege didn't seem so assured, and observing her ambitious determination to see the world and make her place in it (Munich was just her first stop), she seemed to be planning to make sure that one day it would be. Instinctively, she sensed that the table was central to her efforts.

What put me onto this train of thought is the real estate market, which has gone right through the roof lately where we live. Condo development, in particular, is on the rise, and I notice that in most of the contemporary layouts, certainly the one-bedroom condos, space for dining is completely left out, unless you count the space at the kitchen counter where two stools might go. Kitchens themselves are shrinking in condos, often reduced to nothing more than parking spots for a coffee machine and a microwave. I suppose the logic is: nobody wants to cook. And, by extension, nobody wants to eat, at least not properly.

This is a slippery slope, and I'm sure my long-lost friend Gina would agree. Whether or not we habitually cook and sit down to eat, we must remember that a dining table is never just a table. It's also a billboard that reflects back at us what our standards are for how we expect to live, and for what we believe we deserve. It's also a place where we communicate to others how we expect them to behave and to treat us as well as one another. In short, tables talk. And it's worth listening to them, because whatever story it is they're telling us, they're telling it three times a day.

I've never been a fan of the self-help genre, but if I were to add a chapter to it, I'd focus on the saving graces of a table. I certainly wish a proper dining space on absolutely everyone, especially anyone living in what might be considered unfortunate circumstances. Even if all you had was a tray to work with, you could start to change the story of your life: a solid tray, carrying a lovely plate, cloth napkin, proper eating implements, a glass, a candle, perhaps a beaker-sized glass containing a daisy plucked from the side of the road. Never underestimate the value of it. A table, however small, and even if there's only room for one, is enough to make good on a promise every day: a promise of beauty, hope, sustenance, and at least some measure of power and position in the world.

Veal Chops with Prunes

Gina would have gone mad for a dish like this, darkly rich, with a perfect balance of fruity acid and sweet. Start soaking the prunes early in the day, and bring the chops to room temperature for an hour before you cook them. Apart from those two minor gestures, this is a dish that can be on the table in under thirty minutes and that tastes of absolute luxury. Note that it can also be made with pork chops or pork tenderloin, if you prefer.

SERVES 4

12 prunes

1¼ cups/300 ml red wine

¾ cup/175 ml good-quality brown stock

2 veal chops (about 14 ounces/390 g each)

Salt and pepper

A thread of neutral oil, for frying

⅓ cup/75 ml crème fraîche (or half sour cream and half heavy
   cream)

1 tablespoon butter

A handful of chopped fresh flat-leaf parsley

Early in the day, put the prunes in a bowl, pour in the wine, and leave to soak. At suppertime, simmer them in the wine for 5 minutes in a small saucepan, then remove the prunes with a slotted spoon and reserve. Pour the stock into the wine, and boil to reduce to ¾ cup/175 ml.

Heat the oven to 350°F/180°C. Season the chops well with salt and pepper. Heat a little oil in an ovenproof frying pan and fry the chops until golden and partially cooked through, about 2 minutes per side. Transfer the chops to the oven to finish cooking, about 8 minutes, then move the chops to a cutting board, cover loosely with foil, and let rest for another 8 minutes.

Continued on the next page

Pour the cooking oil out of the pan, leaving behind any nice sticky bits. Pour the wine mixture into the pan and add the crème fraiche. Boil down to sauce consistency. Remove from the heat and whisk in the butter to make the sauce glossy. Taste and season with salt and pepper.

Put the prunes into the sauce to heat through. Slice the chops. Pour the sauce onto a serving platter, arrange the sliced chops on top, and scatter over the parsley. Serve immediately.

Marquise au Chocolat

Here's a dessert with what you might call presence, especially if you dust the top with icing sugar and powdered gold leaf. In cookbooks from the 1980s, when it was popular, you see it served with raspberry coulis or custard sauce. We prefer it with a dollop of crème fraîche, or equal parts heavy cream and sour cream whipped together. I also like to surround it with a galaxy of physalis when I can get my hands on those lovely, little golden fruits.

MAKES ONE 11½ × 4½-INCH/29 × 11-CM TERRINE

12 ounces/330 g 70% chocolate, chopped

1¼ cups/285 g unsalted butter, chopped

¼ cup/30 g cocoa powder

2 tablespoons espresso

4 large egg whites and 3 large egg yolks

Pinch of salt

½ cup/75 g icing sugar

1⅓ cups/325 ml heavy cream, cold

Line a large terrine with plastic wrap.

Put the chocolate, butter, and cocoa powder in a metal bowl set over a pot of simmering water and gently melt. Stir in the espresso.

Whisk the egg whites to firm peaks with the salt. In a separate bowl, beat the egg yolks and icing sugar until thick and pale. In another bowl, whip the cream.

First, fold the whites into the yolk mixture. Next, fold in the chocolate mixture, followed by the cream. Pour into the terrine, cover, and chill overnight.

To serve, unmould and remove the wrap. Let the marquise sit for 30 minutes to take the chill off before slicing with a hot knife.

29

Dream Kitchen

I remember visiting a three-star restaurant in central France one time and being dumb-struck when I toured the kitchen, because you could have heard a pin drop. All the cooks were calmly and quietly doing their thing, one picking the leaves off stems of herbs, another plucking a pheasant, another pressing pastry into tart shells with the tenderness of a mother tucking her baby into bed . . . tum dee dum dum . . . With no loud music, no yelling, no fast moves, that kitchen had the peaceful sanctity of a Buddhist temple. This must have had an effect on the food, because it was some of the most delicious and elegant I've ever eaten.

Ah, the serene kitchen. It's easy to forget such a thing can exist; certainly there's a paucity of images of them in the media. Think of all the television competition shows where the contestants scramble around in a frantic state of tension, terrified that their maple mousse might not set on time or that they'll accidentally undercook a lentil.

Think too of the advertising directed at home cooks, showing them harried and defeated as they face yet another chocolate-milk spill or discover a forgotten pot of rice pudding on the stove with a charred black bottom. And the solutions offered to offset moments of distress? Just the other day, I came across an article citing a list of gadgets that promise to take the stress out of cooking, amongst them a Ninja pressure cooker, a rapid egg cooker, and "shredding claws." Sheesh! How about a glass of Sancerre and a little bit of Bach instead?

We all experience moments of stress in the kitchen. Schedules get overloaded, we get overtired or "over-peopled," other priorities that make cooking feel like an interruption get in the way. There's no denying it, but aligning ourselves with these negative states for any length of time never helps. Just last week I was hosting a birthday party and decided that the "cake" should be pavlova. We were to be quite a crowd, so I'd need two and I decided to knock them both off at once, doubling the recipe and baking them on a single sheet pan. For whatever reason, I used a recipe that wasn't my usual, and, for whatever reason, after the full baking time in the oven they were like giant marshmallows, but with no crisp exterior whatsoever. Was it the recipe, my doubling of it, the weather? A mystery. Anyway, I had no choice but to ditch them both and start again, and I was determined not to get flustered. This time I used my own recipe and made just one pavlova. After an hour in the oven, it was perfect, so I turned off the heat and left it in there while I went about other things. An hour later, I returned to take it out only to realize that I'd merely turned off the timer and not the heat, so now my perfect pavlova was brown, crinkled, and split. Into the bin went that one, too. I think I actually screamed at this point, one of those blood-curdling howls that is truly an act of violence against one's own throat and not recommended. Of course, afterwards I felt like an idiot and had to ask myself: What kind of cook do you want to be and what kind of kitchen do you want around you? After a deep breath (or ten), I launched into pavlova number four, and then decided to make a chocolate cake for the second dessert because, by then, if I'd used more egg whites I'd have had enough leftover yolks to make mayonnaise for a cruise ship.

Nobody ever talks about their dream living room, but everybody and his hound dog hankers after a dream kitchen. Well, my dream kitchen, I've decided, whatever it might look like, is a serene kitchen, and ever since the pavlova incident I've been putting more thought into how to get one. There's the obvious: tear out the current kitchen and replace it. But, that's not a sensible thing to do at the moment and, besides, you can't really blame things like a botched pavlova on a creaky cupboard door or outmoded flooring. The problem is me.

I remember a Russian friend in Paris once racing over to another friend's stovetop and turning down the heat on a pot of potatoes. She was horrified. "You don't boil potatoes, you brute, you simmer them!" That stuck with me, because I'd never thought before about the importance of cooking gently, not just for the sake of one's food, but for one's own nervous system. I'm mindful about that now, washing citrus fruits with a loving rub, laying steak out carefully on the counter rather than slapping it down, even pounding anchovies in a mortar and pestle more with the force of a masseuse than that of a prisoner breaking rocks. I like to think the food responds better to me when I handle it like that. My mood sure does.

It's also important, or so I'm telling myself, to remember to move breezily and easily around a kitchen, not to lunge and plunge clumsily about, and not to speed. Cook more like a ballerina, in other words, rather than a raging bull let loose in a Limoges factory. It reminds me of the time I was told by a French boyfriend not to walk so fast (the same boyfriend I had dinner with at the aforementioned restaurant where the kitchen was so calm). "Why not?" I asked defensively. The reply was one only a Frenchman could give: "C'est inélégant."

You don't see the words "kitchen" and "elegance" in the same sentence any more often than you do the words "kitchen" and "serene," but thinking about achieving serenity, elegance does suggest itself. After all, isn't elegance about finding perfect balance, doing not too little and not too much? It also gives an admirable appearance of effortlessness and expertise. Think of the fight scenes in kung fu movies: the evil villain is always shown thrashing around like a windmill, then the hero comes along and brings him to his knees with nothing but a flick of the wrist. Elegant. And, of course, the hero walks away with all the serenity of a swan gliding across a glass-still lake.

With all this talk of becoming the serene queen of my inner cuisine, I actually am starting mentally to plan a nuts-and-bolts kitchen renovation. I'm inspired by a few Korean YouTubers for how I want it to feel. Their videos are slow and meditative, never even showing a face, just the mindful and carefree motions of rice spilling into a lovely clay pot to cook; vegetables being julienned by a relaxed, unhurried hand; washed fruit draining on a large "platter" made of basketweave . . . Once in a while they'll pan the camera over to catch a few Zen moments of raindrops hitting the kitchen window or ripe juice-heavy lemons hanging from an indoor tree. Cook and kitchen become inseparable when things are serene. There's the ultimate dream.

Beef Cheeks Braised in Red Wine Sauce

There's nothing dreamier than walking into a house filled with the scent of something braising in wine, and this simple and relatively inexpensive dish will give you just that. Braised beef cheeks are soft and yielding in texture, compared to regular stew meat, and they're delicious served on a purée of parsnip or celeriac to keep things cloud-like.

SERVES 6

2 tablespoons olive oil, plus more as needed

2 pounds/900 g beef cheeks (3 to 4)

Salt and pepper

1 medium onion, sliced

1 carrot, sliced

1 celery rib, sliced

2 cups/250 ml red wine

1 bouquet garni (a few sprigs each of fresh thyme and flat-leaf parsley, plus a bay leaf)

2 cups/500 ml beef stock

A handful of finely chopped fresh flat-leaf parsley leaves

Heat the oven to 325°F/160°C.

Heat the oil in a Dutch oven. Season the meat with salt and pepper, and, working in batches if necessary, brown very well on both sides, about 5 minutes total per cheek. Remove, and set aside. Add the onion, carrot, and celery to the pot, along with a drizzle more of oil, if needed, and cook, stirring occasionally, until starting to brown, about 5 minutes. Deglaze with the wine, drop in the bouquet garni, return the meat to the pot, add the stock and, if needed, add a little water to cover. Lay a piece of parchment paper on top of the stew, then cover with a tight-fitting lid, transfer to the oven, and cook for 2½ hours.

Remove from the oven, discard the parchment, and transfer the meat with a slotted spoon to a holding dish. Strain the braising liquid, discarding the vegetables and bouquet garni, then return the liquid to the pot, bring to a boil, and reduce until thick, 1 cup/250 ml to 1½ cups/375 ml. Return the meat to the pot, cover, and set aside. Reheat and sprinkle with the chopped parsley to serve.

Parsnip Purée

Impossibly, pillowy light in feel, but secretly rich as blazes.

SERVES 4 TO 6

2 pounds/900 g parsnips, peeled and sliced
½ cup/125 ml milk
Salt
½ cup/110 g butter, cut into pieces
½ cup/125 ml cream
Pepper

Put the parsnips and milk in a pot, add water to cover, season with salt, then bring to a boil and simmer until the parsnips are very tender, 10 to 15 minutes, depending on size. Drain. Whizz in a food processor with the butter and cream, taste, and season with salt and pepper.

Quick Zucchini Pickle

Braised meats, stews, and meat pies alike are all perked up with a spoonful of this colourful, vinegary pickle on the side, which is why I always have it in the pantry. To sterilize jars and lids, simply run them through the dishwasher, or set just-washed (but not dried) jars upside down on a baking sheet and pop them into a 350°F/180°C oven for 15 minutes. Meanwhile, pour boiling water over the lids (and funnel, if you're using one) in a bowl and fish them out with tongs when you're ready to use them.

MAKES 6 PINTS

3 pounds/1.35 kg zucchini, thinly sliced (about 10 cups)

1 large onion, finely chopped (around 1 pound/450 g)

1 large red bell pepper, finely diced

5 tablespoons pickling salt

3 cups/600 g sugar

2½ cups/625 ml white vinegar

2 tablespoons cornstarch

2 teaspoons celery seed

2 teaspoons mustard seed

1 teaspoon ground turmeric

Put the zucchini, onion, bell pepper, and pickling salt in a large bowl. Toss to coat, cover with cold water, and let sit on the countertop overnight.

The next day, drain off the liquid and put the vegetables in a large pot. Add the sugar, vinegar, cornstarch, celery seed, mustard seed, and turmeric. Bring to a boil, and simmer for 20 minutes.

Spoon the hot mixture into sterilized jars. Screw the lids on tight. No refrigeration is required until after opening.

30

Dressed for Dinner

"There is no greater sight than a properly laid dinner table," wrote Arthur Inch, an English butler who acted as an advisor for the film *Gosford Park*. I could not agree more, which is why I am glad to see the minimalist trend in tabletop décor finally take a backseat and make way for the current surge in what the late Sir Terence Conran dubbed "tablescapes." How interesting that an obsession with this domestic art should have begun its upswing during a global pandemic, a time when we all had to curtail our entertaining so drastically. I guess there's a natural inclination during times of restriction to want to go all out.

It's like deciding to go on a diet and immediately being struck by a craving for Doritos and Oreos. The subconscious mind doesn't like to be told "no." This must explain why tables set with things like stark white plates and utilitarian mason jars to drink from are on the outs. (Good riddance. I've always found the monastic aesthetic strangely pretentious.) Meanwhile, incoming are dining tables that are veritable pageants of gown-length table linens; woven chargers; colourful, twisted, hand-dipped candles; tin soldiers or Chinese urns; botanical gardens' worth of cascading flower bouquets; ripe fruit displayed on pedestalled serving bowls. "Whatever may become of us tomorrow," these tables seem to say, "tonight we dine!"

Something else I've noticed is that tabletop is blurring more with fashion lately. All the big houses like Dior and Hermès are going full steam ahead with their home lines, and every influencer in the land seems to be as keen on showing off her latest table accessories— camouflage-print cutlery, circus-scene dinner plates, mouth-blown Murano glasses—as she is her cross-body handbags and rattan earrings. Some designers have even gone so far as to coordinate their collections of dresses and table linens, so that the line between hostess and table is a blur. Putting all this together, I'm realizing that how we dress our tables says as much about who we are—and how we are—as does the way we dress ourselves.

I have to confess that I have always been somewhat deficient in the clothing department. I do make an effort to dress properly, but I've never had any great sense of style. It doesn't help that I loathe clothes shopping and have always had the smallest closets of anyone I know. I remember a friend who worked for *Vogue* once walking into a bedroom I had in Paris, taking one look at the closet, and flatly declaring, "That's a problem." It still is, I'm afraid, but at least now it's finally starting to bother me, so perhaps I'll do something about it. And, while I'm at it, I want to do something about my table wardrobe, too.

I don't think Mr. Inch, the butler, actually had style on his mind when he wrote about his fondness for a properly set table. Surely he was referring to correctness: having the crystal polished, the monograms on the plates right side up, the cutlery in all the right places, the chairs all in even alignment. His career would have spanned two world wars, so I can see why this must have mattered to him so much. There's something reassuring about finding a table ready to receive you when you arrive at it, with everything in its proper place and in proper condition: merciful order at the heart of madness. Well, even the simplest of table settings can achieve this, just as the simplest dress, as long as it's neat and fits, can have a calming effect on its wearer. But right now we must be craving more than mere correctness when we come to the table.

I had a friend in school who, on days when he got out of the wrong side of the bed, wore what he called his "bad day shirt," a rather ugly brown- and mustard-coloured rag with flecks of purple in it. The only good thing about it was that the rest of us, when we saw him coming down the hall, at least had fair warning as to what mood to expect out of him. But it was a misguided tactic, because when the chips are down, we should put even greater effort into dressing up!

Some people have a habit of dressing for dinner every night. You could write that off as preposterously swanky, but when you think about the positive effect it can have on the psyche, it's really not a bad idea. For a while during the pandemic, as a rebellion against the concept of "casual Friday," and as a complete rejection of succumbing to "pyjama paralysis," Peter and I rose to a self-imposed weekly occasion we dubbed "Fancy Friday." It was just the two of us for dinner, but so what? We put on our best, raised a glass to each other, and dined on something that made the dressing up feel worthwhile.

I've never been one to follow trends, but I'm keen on this tabletop turn of events. For the past few years, dinner really has felt like the highlight of every day. So, on that note, I'll deck the table and deck myself, too. Whatever may come of us tomorrow, tonight we dine!

Glazed Duck with Turnips and Celery Hearts

Turnips are a classic French pairing with duck, but this salty-sweet sauce lends an exotic twist. Be sure to buy a head of celery with plenty of leaves because their feathery freshness cuts the richness in a lovely way. This is an easy recipe, but it does take some judgement: be sure to factor in the size of your duck breast and test the turnips as they're cooking, because timing will depend on the size of those too.

SERVES 4 AS A FIRST COURSE OR 2 AS A MAIN COURSE

1 large duck breast or two small (about 1 pound/450 g)

Zest and juice of a large orange (about ½ cup/125 ml juice)

¼ cup/60 ml soy sauce

3 tablespoons honey, divided

3 tablespoons butter, divided

1 pound/450 g medium-small turnips, peeled and cut into wedges

Salt and pepper

Leaves and the thinly sliced pale innermost stalk from a bunch of celery

Heat the oven to 450°F/230°C.

Score the fat on the duck breast, then lay the breast, fat side down, in a cold ovenproof frying pan. Set aside. Mix together the orange zest and juice, soy sauce, and 2 tablespoons of the honey. Set aside. Put the turnips, 1 tablespoon of the butter, and the remaining tablespoon of honey in a frying pan that fits them in a single layer. Season with salt and pepper, and add water just to cover. Set aside on the stovetop.

Set the duck over medium-low heat and render off all but about ¼ inch/6 mm of fat, about 10 minutes. (Reserve the melted fat for another use, such

Continued on the next page

as duck fat–roasted potatoes). Increase the heat under the duck to medium and brown the fat side, about 3 minutes. Once the fat is golden and crisp, pour away any remaining melted fat from the pan, and flip the breast to its fat side up. Pour the reserved orange juice mixture over the meat, and transfer to the oven. Cook to medium rare, no higher than 130°F/54°C, about 8 minutes.

While the duck is in the oven, bring the turnips to a boil, then reduce the heat and simmer until the liquid has evaporated and the turnips are tender, 10 to 15 minutes. If the pan goes dry before they're done, add a little more water, and at the end, turn the turnips a few times to get the wedges golden on both sides. When the duck is cooked, remove it from the oven and let it rest, uncovered, for about 10 minutes. Set the pan of juices on a burner and boil down by about half, then remove from the heat and whisk in the remaining 2 tablespoons of butter to make a glaze.

Slice the duck. Toss the celery with the turnips and arrange on a platter. Lay the sliced duck alongside, and spoon the glaze over. Serve.

Black Cod with White Wine Sauce, Savoy Cabbage, and Chestnuts

Black cod is a luxuriously buttery fish, gorgeous with this classic wine cream sauce. The cabbage (you can also use brussels sprouts leaves) provides a leafy foil, with added depth from the bacon and fudgy chestnuts. Serve a bowl of buttered, parslied kasha on the side.

SERVES 4

FOR THE FISH

4 pieces of black cod, about 5 ounces/140 g each, skinned

Salt and pepper

1 shallot, minced

1 cup/250 ml white wine

1 teaspoon white wine vinegar

1 cup/250 ml heavy cream

1 teaspoon Cognac

FOR THE CABBAGE

12 ounces/340 g Savoy cabbage or brussels sprouts

2 slices bacon, cut into lardons

2 tablespoons butter

Salt and pepper

12 soft Italian chestnuts, quartered

To make the fish, pat the fish dry with paper towel and season with salt and pepper. Lay on a parchment-lined baking sheet. Set aside. Heat the oven to 400°F/200°C.

Put the shallot and wine in a saucepan, bring to a boil, and reduce to ¼ cup/60 ml. Strain into a large, clean saucepan, discarding the shallot. Add

Continued on the next page

the vinegar and cream. Bring to a boil (the large pan will prevent it from boiling over), and reduce to sauce consistency, about ½ cup/125 ml. Stir in the Cognac, taste, and season with salt and pepper to taste. Keep the sauce warm.

To make the cabbage, remove the ribs from the cabbage and cut into roughly 2-inch pieces. Alternatively, remove the leaves from the brussels sprouts, discarding the cores. Put the bacon into a cold frying pan, and fry until cooked. Remove to paper towel. Add the butter and cabbage to the pan, season with salt and pepper, cover, and sweat the cabbage until it is tender. Add the chestnuts, along with the bacon, to heat through.

Pop the fish into the oven and cook until the flesh is opaque (130°F/54°C on a thermometer), 10 to 15 minutes. Transfer the cabbage or sprouts to a serving dish. Pour the hot sauce into another warm serving dish and lay in the fish. Serve immediately.

31

Cottage Cookery

"We should not be doing this," Peter said, shaking his head, as we sat trapped in impatient traffic one Sunday on our way to the grocery store. "This should be a day off. You do nothing but read, take a walk, listen to the birds, have a pink gin and tonic in the middle of the afternoon outside . . . " We were both worn out from the workweek and what he said was true, but it's almost impossible in a 24/7 world to put a foot down and say, in effect, "Sorry, I'm closed." Unless, of course, it's August, which is why I'm counting the days for the month to arrive. Get me out of Dodge, give me nature, give me peace, and slow me down to a country-cooking kind of pace.

Everything tastes better in August, and not just because vegetable gardens are in full swing. It's something to do with the kind of food we cook to late summer's rhythms. I think of what it's like at my mother-in-law's summer house in Métis-sur-Mer on the Gaspé Peninsula. There, unless you're an avid golfer, tennis player, or bridge afficionado (we are not), there is strictly nothing to do, apart from walk the stoney shoreline collecting colourful, sea-smoothed beach glass like magpies. Or you can mosey down to the one and only grocery shop in town, run by a man called Monsieur Ratté, and see what's on offer. Mostly, he carries the usual cottage essentials like marshmallows, ketchup, and beer, but he also has a tiny selection of locally grown vegetables; seafood, including lobster, scallops, and itty-bitty crevettes de Matane; plus some meats which he butchers himself. It's amazing how effortless a dinner plan becomes once you don't have to navigate your way through a supermarket the size of an oil tanker. Walking home from Ratté's with a modest selection, I'll have a menu planned before I'm through the front door: corn chowder, lobster rolls, blueberry buckle. Done. It sounds counterintuitive, but the restricted choice of ingredients you have to work with in cottage country can actually be an inspiration, rather than a drawback, as can having supplies occasionally run low. I remember one summer getting down to a head of celery and an apple in the crisper, and it led to the creation of a most delicious celery Vichyssoise. I'd never have come up with that in the city.

Something else I love about cooking in the country is that you can get back to recipes that for some reason seem a bit out of place in an urban environment. In the kitchen at my parents' house, I never feel the pressure to try to be exotic. Pound cake can be pound cake. I don't have to add matcha to it not to look old-school. Baked beans are allowed, served with chow chow and Johnny cake. I wouldn't dare set that on a table in the city, although I'm not sure why. "To thine own self be true/and it must follow, as the night the day/thou canst not then be false to any man." (As said Polonius in *Hamlet*.) It can be as challenging to stick to that bit of advice as it is to set a Sunday aside for doing nothing.

I'm now remembering an unexpectedly delicious dish called "Beer

Can Chicken," which was served by a friend at her lakeside cottage one summer. That's the recipe in which you prop a bird up on an open can of lager and put it on the grill so that, as the chicken cooks and its skin crispens, the beer steams the inside, keeping the meat moist. Somehow that strikes me as a dish that wouldn't taste quite the same without a few pine trees swaying overhead while you ate it. As children, back when watermelons still had seeds, my brothers and I used to have great fun with seed-spitting contests: we'd stand on the deck facing the river and see who could torpedo their seeds the farthest as we munched down our giant pink wedges and let the juice run down our chins. In cottage country, you can get away with making birthday cake from a store-bought mix and covering it in a colourful fireworks of sprinkles. Nobody will bat an eye or accuse you of laziness or bad taste.

My sister-in-law recently gave me a book put together by members of the Cascade Golf and Tennis Club in Métis-sur-Mer. It's called *Summer Cooks . . . and Some Are Not*. (Cottage humour.) It's packed with recipes for an audience adjusted to August, so you can make them without having to stick your tongue in your cheek. There's one for smoked oysters with cream cheese and chili on cucumber slices for the cocktail hour, another for chicken and vegetable casserole in cheesy cream sauce topped with biscuits, and another for pasta salad containing, amongst other things, tinned mandarin oranges (I'd forgotten they even existed!). Something called Monkey Bars, packed with cookie crumbs, banana chips, chocolate chips, peanut butter chips, roasted peanuts, and sweetened condensed milk, is not anything I'd ever eat, but, you know, as I look forward to August, maybe what the heck! At the cottage, you get to cook—and eat—like nobody's looking.

I've always found it rather irritating when people come back from holidaying in Europe and wax on about how glorious the architecture is, how civilized the meals, and how smartly dressed the people, but then don't do anything to try to create any of that loveliness themselves at home. Perhaps they have no imagination or it all feels too overwhelming, even impossible, but I always think, "Couldn't they try?" This, of course, points the finger right back at me, because if I love country cooking so much, then why can't I figure out its secret ingredient so that I can bring it back home to my kitchen in the city? I moaned to Peter about this, but he wasn't on my side. "Embrace the difference," he said. "A big part of what you love about cooking in the country is that it's a change." I suppose he's right.

Celery Vichyssoise

A refreshing soup for summer.

3 tablespoons butter

1 onion, chopped

1 bunch of celery (about 1½ pounds/675 g), chopped

1 medium potato, peeled and chopped

1 apple, peeled, cored, and chopped

4 cups/1 litre chicken stock

Salt and pepper

Chopped fresh chives, for serving

Heat the butter in a saucepan and gently sauté the onion and celery until soft, 15 to 20 minutes. Add the potato and apple, pour in the chicken stock, season with salt and pepper, bring to a simmer, and cook until the vegetables and apple are very soft, about half an hour.

Once everything is soft, let cool a little, then purée in a blender, and strain. Taste, adjust the thickness with a little more stock, if needed, and check the seasonings. Serve warm or chilled with chopped chives on top.

Plum Clafoutis for High Summer

This crowd-pleasing, cake-like pudding, loaded with juicy fruit, comes from a friend who has an enviable apple orchard for producing her own cider and also has several plum trees. I get a sack of them from her every year so I can make this.

SERVES 6 TO 8

½ cup/110 g butter, softened

¾ cup/150 g sugar, plus more for garnish

3 eggs, lightly beaten

Pinch of salt

1 teaspoon vanilla

1 tablespoon Cointreau

Zest of 1 orange

1 cup/125 g flour

3 cups/800 g halved, pitted plums

Heat the oven to 350°F/180°C.

Cream together the butter and sugar, then beat in the eggs, salt, vanilla, Cointreau, and orange zest. Finally, mix in the flour. Pour into a pie plate or baking dish, and distribute the plums evenly over top. Sprinkle over some extra sugar for garnish, and bake until the batter is set, about 45 minutes.

Serve warm or at room temperature.

32

Dessert Be Damned

I may first have realized that sweets were not especially my cup of tea the year I spent in Munich in my twenties. The multitude of cafés and confectionery shops certainly impressed me, bursting at the seams as they were with delectable-looking plum tarts, apple strudels, cream-stuffed doughnuts, marzipan animals, cheesecakes, iced cakes with variously flavoured creams between every layer, roulades, puff pastry concoctions. It was jaw-dropping, and for more than one reason. Every time I passed a window with sweets on display, I wondered in disbelief who on earth would actually eat them all. Then, mid-afternoon every day, I'd be reminded, because from out of nowhere people would suddenly flood the streets and pack every empty café chair in the land, ready to tuck into gigantic slabs of Schokoladentorte and Mokkaschnitten. How there was a single skinny person in Germany was beyond me, but perhaps the trick was that they indulged in their cake eating between meals, rather than tacking it on to the end of dinner at night. I myself never partook.

All I ever wanted to buy were the large, yeasty pretzels with their shiny dark-brown crust, freckled with coarse salt (Brezeln). What can I say, I'm a savoury sort!

And, thankfully, most of my close friends are like me in this respect, a relief when it comes to dinner parties because, having come to this realization over time, most of us have now axed the dreaded dessert course from our menus altogether. Why bother going to the trouble to produce a praline-topped coffee roly-poly cake or a marquise au chocolat decorated in gold leaf if they're only going to be looked at from afar and never eaten? And yet, it would feel wrong to end a meal abruptly, bringing down the curtain on supper immediately after the meat and potatoes act. Dessert does serve as a denouement, which is an important part of a meal's rhythm, so one has to find alternatives.

One friend's solution is to offer a cheese course in place of dessert, setting out a few contrasting varieties along with some nuts, thin wafers, and perhaps a bowl of clementines. Another is keen on serving solo scoops of sorbet, which many would consider a mere palate cleanser but for me make a perfect punctuation mark to any meal. I've got my "Japanese oranges" trick, an idea I pinched from a sushi restaurant one time. It's a way of cutting the fruit so that you end up with orange sections served in "bowls" that you make out of the peel.

Sugar lovers take a completely different approach to their dinner finales. Not only do they produce dessert without fail, but often they'll turn it into the menu's pièce de résistance. These are people for whom no feast of barbecued pork ribs and cobs of corn is complete without their signature peanut butter cheesecake to round it out (ouf!) . . . or their rice pudding or maple bread pudding or coconut cream pie. "Just a little sliver for me," I'll beg meekly, but sweet tooths don't have it in them to be parsimonious, at least not when it comes to their beloved desserts. So I brace myself as a hugely generous slab of something—a wedge of chocolate snowball, a brick of semifreddo—lands before me, and after a few obligatory bites, though the taste may be divine, I'm afraid I have to lay down my fork. I do feel some guilt about this, because the effort people put into these masterpieces is commendable, and it must be terribly disappointing when a guest doesn't share their host's enthusiasm.

The word "dessert" comes from the French "desservir," de-serve, which refers to clearing the table. Back when people were still dining à la française, which meant that a variety of dishes for any meal were placed on the table at the same time for people to share, the table got de-served (i.e., cleared) all at once, to make way for palate-cleansing tidbits like fruits, nuts, and sweetmeats. That's how the word "dessert" became associated with things sweet. Then, when Europe switched to service à la russe, which divided meals into separate courses, dessert apparently acquired equal rank to all the other courses. Does this mean we went from expecting a few candied orange rinds after our wild boar to feeling ripped off if an iced cake the size of a Greek temple didn't appear?

I hate to sound like a party pooper (and I know that no party is a party without dessert), but given how often I have accommodated other people's food preferences and dislikes, I do rather feel entitled to this particular quirk of my own. Some people are allergic to gluten, others to fish or shellfish, some have a dairy intolerance, others dislike garlic or peas, many won't touch pork, there are an increasing number of vegans . . . Well, I'm afraid I'm dessert intolerant, unless it's being offered in the merciful size of a canapé. Happily, yet another friend has started catering to this preference, turning dessert into a minor buffet of tiny squares of almond cake, slices of pineapple, bowls of candied ginger, physalis, strawberries, licorice, high-end candies, and chocolates. It is sweet stuff, and with plenty of variety, but in only itty-bitty portions, none of which is forced on anyone. That with a cup of herbal tea is a finale of which even I have become a fan.

Japanese Oranges

This is my favourite way to eat oranges, and a perfect dessert for when you don't really want any. Plan on a half orange per person.

Slice the ends off the oranges to expose the flesh, and reserve them. Cut the resulting orange "barrel" in half so you have two rounds. Slide a sharp knife between the flesh and the peel and cut around so that you have two rings of rind and two wheels of fruit. Set each ring of rind on end, like a bottomless bowl, then lay in the reserved ends to give the bowls their bases. Finally, cut the fruit into 6 to 8 sections each, trim off any white pith, and arrange in the orange-rind dishes. Cover and chill.

To serve, arrange on a platter and stick bamboo skewers or toothpicks into the fruit for eating. It's nice to have some coins of candied ginger and some chocolates to serve at the same time.

Coffee Roll with Hazelnut Praline

I am no pastry chef, so it always thrills me when I can produce a cake that looks fancy but is in fact child's play to make. This soft coffee-scented sponge, filled with coffee cream and garnished with praline, is just such an achievement. It's impressive to look at, and at the same time light, so it's ideal for serving after a festive meal. An added bonus: it can be made with gluten-free flour.

SERVES 8 TO 10

FOR THE SPONGE

5 eggs, separated and at room temperature

Pinch of salt

⅓ cup/75 g sugar

¼ cup/60 ml strong espresso

⅓ cup/75 ml grapeseed oil

½ cup/60 g cake flour or cornstarch, sifted

Icing sugar, for dusting

FOR THE FILLING

1½ cups/375 ml heavy cream, divided

1 tablespoon espresso powder

1½ tablespoons sugar

A few drops of vanilla

FOR THE PRALINE

¼ cup/60 ml water

½ cup/100 g sugar

½ cup/60 g hazelnuts or pecans

Heat the oven to 350°F/180°C. Line a 15½ × 10-inch/39 × 27-cm jelly-roll tin with parchment. Put a metal bowl in the freezer for whipping cream.

For the sponge, using electric beaters, beat the egg whites to soft peaks with the salt, then gradually beat in the sugar a little at a time. Set aside. In another bowl, beat the egg yolks until thick and ribbony, then beat in the espresso, followed by the oil, and finally the flour or cornstarch. Gently fold some of the whites into the yolk mixture to loosen it up, then fold in the rest. Pour into the prepared pan and bake until a toothpick inserted in the centre comes out clean, 15 to 18 minutes.

Remove from the oven and slide the cake off the pan. Lay a piece of parchment on top and flip the cake over. Peel the parchment that it baked on gently away from the cake, and flip back over. Cool completely.

For the filling, put ½ cup/125 ml of the cream in a saucepan with the espresso powder and heat to dissolve. Pour into a cup and place in the freezer to cool down. Once the mixture is very cold, remove the chilled whisking bowl from the freezer and pour the cool coffee cream into it. Add the remaining cream, along with the sugar and vanilla, and whisk to stiff peaks.

Spread the coffee cream over the cake, leaving a finger's width uncovered along one long side. Gently roll up the log in the direction of the side of the cake with the uncovered margin, and slide onto a serving platter. Refrigerate for at least 30 minutes to firm.

For the praline, cover a baking sheet with parchment and set aside. Put the water and sugar in a saucepan and bring to a boil. Cook to golden caramel, swirling the pan occasionally once it's liquid and not letting it get too dark. Remove from the heat, stir in the nuts, and pour onto the parchment, tilting the pan so the praline spills into a thin sheet. Set aside to harden, then transfer to a cutting board, and chop.

To serve the cake, remove the roll from the refrigerator, dust with icing sugar, and decorate the top with the praline. Slice to serve, or refrigerate until serving.

33

Feeling Greens

The leaf blowers are back. No sooner are the daffodils up and have the robins returned than out come those reverse outdoor vacuums, roaring down the lane as loud as so many 747s taking off, to blast at every cut blade of grass, dropped flower petal, and fallen leaf. You have to wonder how the poor plants feel. Isn't it classical music they're meant to like?

I was lucky to grow up on a property that didn't go in for loud upkeep machinery. The lawn got mowed, but that was about it, and I'm sure if my parents could have installed a few sheep instead, they'd have preferred it, as would I, because nothing beats the look of a meadow munched as short as a crew cut by calm, grazing animals. We didn't go in for any pesticides either, because as soon my mother looked out the window after a long winter and spotted a dandelion leaf all she could think was "Lunch!" We had to keep our green stuff clean.

Now that I think about it, I'll bet there was a whole lot more to eat all around us that we didn't even know about. A farmer from a few miles up was recently saying that he'd been paid a visit by a Syrian family who wanted to buy milk for making cheese, and when afterwards they'd inspected his garden what they lit right onto was not his vegetables, but his weeds! I wonder which weed it was that caught their attention. What would they do with it? I must know, because there can be no such thing as too many greens. They're my favourite food and, especially in spring, my constant craving.

You used to hear people talk about spring tonics, which could be made from bitter leaves and roots both, not just of dandelions, but also of nettles, chickweed, curly dock, ramps, and the like. After months on a snowy diet of meat and potatoes, pickles and preserves, a welcome tonic was meant to stimulate digestion and circulation, purify the blood and the liver, and generally boost one's health. Some people these days "juice" all year long, but the nutritional value of store-bought kale and Granny Smiths can't possibly hold a candle to what you'd have got from a field of wild things. I remember as a child going out with my father in rubber boots, once the freshet from the river had receded, to gather fiddleheads down by the brook. They're not actually all that much to my liking, but there's always a special thrill to eating anything foraged.

I don't live anywhere near a field right now, but my fridge is nonetheless forever full of different greens. The most industrial I buy are romaine hearts, which I love best with a garlicky lemon dressing and a showering of Parmesan cheese, and also arugula, which I often mix into a salad of lentils, stir through a medley of cooked vegetables, or use as a base for things coming off the barbecue. Looseleaf lettuce is always around for making an acidic salad to follow a roast or stew, and kale is a regular that I shred and mix with apple, nuts, and cheese for a virtuous lunch. In fact, I think I'll have one of those today.

Something like watercress makes a perfect side dish for so many meals, so I buy it when I have a specific intention for it. Butter lettuce, too, feels a bit special because of its delicate nature. It's delicious with green goddess dressing or tucked into sandwiches or used for "bowls" into which to spoon, say, tabbouleh or chicken salad. And, of course, chard and beet greens are routine in this house, the former used in stews or turned into gratin, and the latter, especially when the beets are young, simply blanched or steamed and eaten with loads of butter. Heaven.

Access to all of that should leave nothing for me to complain about, but since greens are a bliss I pine for, there are a few whose absence I lament. Spinach, though obviously available here, is not great quality and has very little taste, so I'm counting the days until I get to France so I can buy the giant stuff that wilts into silky handkerchiefs in butter without ever turning to mush or tasting like mulch. Mâche, those nutty, delicate, dark-green bouquets, is never anywhere to be found in my city, so I'll be delighted to be reunited with that, too, and may have to splash out a fortune on prized walnut oil to celebrate. Ditto nettles. What I would do right now for a basketful to make soup! You can't pick nettles without wearing gloves because, of course, they sting like scorpions, so there's an indication for you of how good they are: people are perfectly happy to gear up to get them. For some reason, frisée and endive are misunderstood in my country. They're supposed to be white, not electric yellow verging on lime green, and they should be big. When you can get them, they're lovely mixed together with a bit of radicchio for an autumn salad with, say, sliced pears, nuts, and a dressing of blue cheese. Frisée is also sturdy enough to stand up to a hot bacon dressing, so that's nice too, and endive leaves are a host's dream because you can fan them out on a platter, top with various things (say tapenade or crushed tangerine), and serve them for appetizers. Oh, and sesame leaves! That's my latest, introduced to me by my Korean sister-in-law. They're also known as shiso leaves, and she uses them to wrap things in such as raw fish or grilled meats. Now my father has started growing them in his garden, thousands of miles away from her native Seoul.

A friend in Paris posted a picture the other day of her haul from L'Agrumiste. Leave it to Paris to have a shop specializing in only citrus fruits! Tangelos, cédrats, kumquats, clementines, Japanese oranges, Bergamot lemons . . . I mean, I haven't heard of half the stuff he carries, but I want it all. This brings to mind another shop I always loved in Paris that specializes in nothing but tinned sardines. You see where I'm heading with this: Wouldn't it be wonderful for a "greens grocer" to spring up? I imagine the owner a spritely, middle-aged man in spectacles and wellies, a connoisseur of everything from puntarella and escarole to purslane and mizuna. You'd walk into his shop and he'd exclaim, "Ah! But, you must try the amaranth today!" or "Allow me to compose for you a customized mesclun mix," which he'd then put together one pinch of greens at a time like a master herbalist.

My insatiable appetite for things green must obviously have something to do with my body's need for certain vitamins or minerals, but I have often argued that vegetables in general are one way of getting close to nature when we're yearning for a dose of it, which everyone is as winter fades out, and especially so anyone living in a city. Perhaps my craving for greens is also that, then: a desire to see the leaves come out on the trees and for the lawn to turn emerald, a yearning for signs of life!

Ironically, one of the best places to find that in a city is in the cemetery. So I think after my lunch of kale salad I may take a walk up there and get some peace from all the lawn and lane weaponry that's busy making a battlefield of the garden. I'll stroll the twisted paths amongst the towering trees, past stretches of emerging spring grass, and be grateful for the music of birdsong rather than blowers, and for all the souls in the ground doing an admirable job pushing up dandelions.

Shredded Kale Salad with Apple, Cheddar, and Almonds

I have made this barely modified *New York Times* recipe more times than I can count, not always with kale but sometimes with spinach or a sturdy, crisp lettuce. It doesn't sound like anything out of the ordinary, but somehow it ends up being more than the sum of its parts. I love it for lunch or whenever I want to feel satisfied but not stuffed.

SERVES 4 AS A FIRST COURSE OR 2 AS A MAIN COURSE

4 cups shredded kale, spinach, or sturdy lettuce (about 3 ounces/
 90 g)

2 tablespoons finely grated Parmesan cheese

¼ cup/20 g sliced almonds (or pumpkin and sunflower seeds),
 toasted

1 apple, cored and diced

2 ounces/60 g aged cheddar cheese, grated

2 tablespoons lemon juice

1 garlic clove, grated

5 tablespoons olive oil

Salt and pepper

Toss the greens with the Parmesan, almonds, apple, and cheddar. Stir together the lemon juice, garlic, and oil, then pour it over the salad. Season with salt and pepper. Toss again thoroughly to coat.

Endive and Radicchio Salad with Apple and Blue Cheese

I've been making the Raymond Blanc version of this classic French salad for years, as well, often improvising on the greens and adding frisée or a handful of watercress. The colourful crunchy bitter leaves mingle with crisp, sweet autumn fruit and walnuts, all veiled in a silky, tangy dressing. It can be served as a first course, but it's also nice after a main course, especially if dessert is going to be something very simple like a plate of cookies. A staple for any salad repertoire.

SERVES 4 TO 6

FOR THE DRESSING
2 ounces/60 g blue cheese, at room temperature
About 1 tablespoon hot water, plus more as needed
1 tablespoon white wine vinegar
2 tablespoons olive oil
Pepper

FOR THE SALAD
1 small head of radicchio, trimmed and quartered lengthwise
1 large endive, cored and quartered lengthwise
1 small apple or ripe pear, thinly sliced
1 celery rib (or the equivalent of celery heart, with leaves), thinly sliced
1 cup/90 g walnuts, roughly chopped
2 ounces/60 g blue cheese, cold
A handful of finely chopped fresh chives

For the dressing, cream the cheese in a small bowl with a fork, then add the warm water to melt slightly. Whisk in the vinegar until smooth, then add the oil and season with pepper. Set aside.

For the salad, put the radicchio, endive, apple, celery, and walnuts into a large bowl. Pour the dressing over, and toss thoroughly to coat the leaves. Transfer to a serving dish, crumble over the blue cheese, scatter over the chives, and serve.

34

A Raison d'Être

What finally got the two-year-old tin of black beans off the bench and into the game was the arrival for dinner of our neighbour, who had in tow one of those people who won't eat anything. We were serving pizza and a salad—gluten-free homemade pizza, even, with Peter's tomato sauce, baby broccoli, red onion, green olives, and a combination of mozzarella and halloumi cheeses. Inoffensive, one would have thought, even for a health nut, but it did not read as edible to our neighbour's friend. So I quickly fried an onion, added a jar of my tomatoes, and stirred in those long-forgotten black beans until hot, then topped the dish with a pile of grated cheddar and set it on the table before the man of delicate appetite, alongside mounds of white rice garnished with fistfuls of fresh coriander. Well, he was pleased as punch, as I think were the beans. It's a terrible thing to sit around interminably waiting for a raison d'être in life. As a friend once observed, "Usefulness restores people," and really that's true of anything. Those beans, now part of a dish, took on a certain glow. In fact, we all ate some.

My heart must be in a different place today, as a result of those beans, because pulling open the dry-goods cupboard this morning, I suddenly noticed a whole load of other ingredients I've been overlooking for a month of Sundays: a box of kasha, a balled-up bag containing an almost countable number of lentils, another with just enough rice with which to make, say, a baby rattle crafted from an empty toilet roll. Who knows how long they've been there, because there are already several other bulging bags and boxes of these same items that have been opened since. Well, this time, instead of ignoring them, I took mercy. I cooked rice, kasha, and lentils, each separately, then forked them all together. Next, I sliced a few onions and fried them to golden threads. To the onion, I added my trio of misfit grains to heat through, then I tossed in chopped pistachios and toasted almonds, handfuls of chopped parsley and dill, dried currants, and grated lemon zest. It was a rags-to-riches story to rival that of Cinderella.

It takes work sometimes to keep our eyes from turning blind to what's right in front of them, or it takes triggers anyway. The threat of houseguests, for instance, always has a wonderful way of causing us suddenly to notice things like the cobwebs that have in fact been draped around the windows like party streamers for weeks, or a powder-room door that won't quite shut anymore. Any state of discomfort, too, is useful for getting us off our butts, as happened to me the other day when I could not concentrate on work and kept hopping up and down out of my chair. After I'd organized the bookshelves, filled a few vases with fresh flowers, and dusted off the diffuser and charged it with lavender water, at last I could sit still and focus. We can only neglect the presence of neglect for so long before it magnifies enough to disturb us into action.

A good example of how this happens in the outside world is with neighbourhoods yet to be beautified. We can glaze over the shabbiness of an area, street after street, for years, until some visionary buys even just one house and fixes it up, putting in new windows with boxes full of blooming geraniums, and repaves the walk. The improvement of this one abode alone suddenly lifts the value of all around it, and lays bare the overlooked potential, which, before long, is realized. Presto: lovely neighbourhood where there wasn't one before! But I digress . . .

It may sound like a stretch, but after that improvised pilaf today, I have become inspired to pay better attention to all the hitherto-ignored store-cupboard items in my kitchen, from the flaked coconut, to the rice-paper wrappers, to the oatmeal of yesteryear. There's an argument that says if we train ourselves to pay attention to the things closest to us that are crying out for our consideration, perhaps we become better people overall, the kind of citizens who spy a weedy, abandoned parking lot and think, "What a perfect place for a labyrinth!" then get to work, rather than just letting it sit there. I see there's an entire bag of sultana raisins in my baking section that obviously didn't choose to crouch unemployed amongst the canisters of baking powder and cocoa for a whole year. It's my fault for not seeing them and helping those raisins find their niche. Why, giving them a "raisin d'être!"

Floating forward from the nether recesses of my brain is something called Uvetta Sotto Spirito, an Italian concoction a friend used to make: raisins macerated for a month in very strong drink. Well, there! You think you're done, finished, and then something suddenly comes along that plumps you up, gives you a new lease on life, hands you a script loaded with fresh things to say and do, and that matter. Everything on earth, we must remember, contains a seed of potential. The tins of coconut milk I don't know what to do with. The endless bags of potato starch (why?!). The Szechuan peppercorns. Me, myself, sometimes, which is why I am perhaps especially grateful to these funny little odds and ends in my kitchen today. Usefulness restores them, just as helping them find their usefulness restores me.

Herbed Rice with Wine and Golden Onion Threads

The wine in this handy rice dish has just the right degree of presence, and the generous addition of arugula and herbs makes it almost a half salad. Delicious both warm and at room temperature.

SERVES 8

¼ cup/60 ml olive oil

1 onion, thinly sliced

1 teaspoon salt, divided

1½ cups/300 g basmati or jasmine rice, rinsed

⅔ cup/150 ml white wine

1⅔ cups/400 ml water or chicken stock

Pepper

A few handfuls of arugula, roughly chopped

Roughly chopped fresh herbs (chives, flat-leaf parsley, coriander, oregano, dill, basil . . .)

Heat the oil in a pot and gently fry the onion, with ½ teaspoon of the salt, until soft and golden, about 20 minutes. Add the rice, pour in the wine and water or stock, and add the remaining salt along with pepper to taste. Cover, and cook until the water has been absorbed, about 10 minutes. Remove the lid, lay a clean tea towel over top of the pot, replace the lid, and set aside for at least another 10 minutes, or longer if you like. The rice will stay hot for a good hour from this point.

To serve, fluff the rice with a fork, and toss with the arugula and herbs.

Tinned Mackerel Salad

I love tinned seafood, everything from smoked oysters to tuna to sardines and, of course mackerel, which for some reason I've been stocking up on lately as if hoarding for the apocalypse. Don't be mistaken, there's nothing lowbrow about the fish, as I believe this salad proves. It's a pretty dish full of exciting tastes, which makes a lovely lunch with some lightly dressed butter lettuce on the side.

SERVES 4

1 pound/450 g new waxy potatoes

Salt

1 pink shallot

¼ cup/60 ml red wine vinegar

1 teaspoon Dijon mustard

Grated zest of 1 lemon

¼ cup/60 ml olive oil

Pepper

2 tins mackerel, 4 ounces/125 g each

2 tablespoons capers

Fresh flat-leaf parsley leaves

Fresh mint leaves

Fresh dill sprigs

Fleur de sel

Put the potatoes in a pot of salted water, bring to a boil, and simmer until tender, about 12 minutes, depending on size. Peel the shallot and slice it into very thin rounds. Place in a bowl, pour the vinegar over, and set aside for 5 minutes. Whisk together the mustard, lemon zest, and olive oil. Season with salt and pepper.

Continued on the next page

When the potatoes are cooked, drain them, rinse in cold water, and slip the skins off. Slice while still warm, arrange flat on a platter, and spoon all but a tablespoon of the dressing evenly over top. Break up the mackerel, removing the spines as you do so, and arrange atop the potatoes. Drain the shallots, discarding the vinegar or saving it for another use, then scatter them over the salad along with the capers, followed by the herbs. Drizzle over the remaining dressing, sprinkle on a little of fleur de sel, and serve.

35

Hosting Goals

I'm not sure where the obsession comes from, but I've always been passionate about entertaining and, in particular, interested in what it takes to be a good host. In the early days, it was all about the cooking. I was ravenous for new recipes and techniques, determined to master every classic from cheese soufflé to red wine sauce, and gung-ho to try every wild idea that was floated under my nose, such as cooking ham in hay, beef in a salt crust, or mussels under a pyre of pine boughs. Today, anything too complicated or odd is of no interest whatsoever. (The three-bird roast, "turducken?" No thanks.) What I strive for now is simplicity, which is actually more difficult, it turns out. I've had some good role models over the years who have shown me that restraint is the ultimate sophistication, so that's the goal. Just as style advisors often recommend looking in the mirror before you leave the house and removing one item of clothing or jewelry to be instantly more chic, I find my menus always improve when

I work up the bravery to delete a dish. My hosting, in this regard, remains a work in progress.

On the heels of my early obsession with the food aspect of entertaining came an appetite for all those things that the French put under the umbrella of l'art de la table: table decoration, familiarity with all the required accoutrements, food presentation, service, and dining etiquette. I have so many books on that stuff, you'd think I ran a catering company or a finishing school. Every rule still fascinates me, too, but thank goodness I did recognize early on that anyone who's not relaxed about them makes a miserable host. I used to know someone like that, so fussed about absolute correctness that he hosted with the stiffness of the tin man. Imagine how distasteful that would have been to someone like Castiglione, the sixteenth-century author of *The Book of the Courtier* who cautioned that one "practice in all things a certain nonchalance that shall conceal design and show that what is done and said is done without effort and almost without thought." He even coined a term for this attitude: sprezzatura.

Later, I started acquiring a number of books about great society hostesses from days of yore, and delving into those it became clear that the success of a Lady Cunard or a Mrs. Vanderbilt never came down merely to her food or whether or not she approved of fish knives, but more to who she managed to get around her table. It's quite hilarious and sometimes horrifying to read about the antics people would get up to trying to snare choice guests for dinner, especially any remotely connected to a crown. I suppose it's still the same today, but that's not my world, so I don't have to worry about it. (A slightly more bohemian lifestyle does have its perks!)

What captured my imagination even more than the great hostesses were the salonnières of seventeenth- and eighteenth-century France. Whether they were any less superficial than their English and American counterparts or not is questionable, but they did at least pretend to have higher ideals than just snagging as many aristocrats and latter-day incarnations of celebrities as they could for their exclusive soirées. The mission of the salonnière (because she had a mission, she wasn't just a party girl) was to gather people for the purpose of engaging in conversation, an art so highly valued at the time that salons were considered essential to upholding the highest standards of social and intellectual life. I always thought that sounded like a noble cause. It made the role of host seem like a serious vocation, not just a hobby, and it gave dinner parties a purpose beyond just having a good time. Not that there's anything wrong with simply enjoying yourself as a host. In fact, that may be the role's greatest challenge. It can be for me.

The French refer to entertaining as l'art de reçevoir, the art of receiving, which puts an interesting spin on things, because when we host, we usually think of ourselves as being on the giving end. Make yourselves at home, eat my food, drink my wine, meet my friends, run me ragged making you happy until you go home, all while I keep my charm turned on full blast. Yikes! Is that how I really feel about it? Not always, no, but sometimes. In fact, a few times I've so exhausted myself trying to be ideal in my hosting (including for unworthy people or people I barely know) that I've ended up going to bed before the party's over. Not that guests have it easy either. It takes energy to be "on" for hours, to be interested in people, witty, good-humoured, sufficiently hungry and generous with praise ... all without making it look like you're having to work at it. Sprezzatura, people!

You'd think I was out to inspire everyone to stay home, lock the doors, and order pizza. But I'm not. It's just that I came across a line of Ralph Waldo Emerson's the other day, "The only gift is a portion of thyself," and it occurred to me that, if it's true, then I've sometimes in fact been a miserly host, not a giver at all, because by the time people have shown up, every last portion of me has been devoured by my trying too hard. "There is no duty we so much underrate as the duty of being happy." That's Robert Louis Stevenson, and he's right, too. We must know how to receive in order truly to give, and it has to start with ourselves.

This, I trust, is the final frontier of my hosting education: to come to grips with the reality that people don't need entertaining, they just want company that makes them feel good, which means that we hosts must make ourselves feel good first in order to receive them. This is a problem I'm now spotting with sprezzatura: it's too much like work to become an expert at studied effortlessness. Why strain to appear blissful and relaxed, when instead you could actually be blissful and relaxed? I take my hosting duties seriously, as you can see. Who ever knew that one's own happiness would turn out to be the priority amongst them. And perhaps, the trickiest one of all to master.

Zucchini Egg Bites

Flavour-packed, savoury bites to serve with drinks, especially good for a cocktail party because they have substance. Note that these are easily made gluten free by simply substituting cornstarch, which has no gluten, for the flour.

MAKES 24 MINI-MUFFIN BITES

1 small zucchini (about ½ pound/225 g)

1 small onion, minced

12 large fresh basil leaves, shredded

12 black olives, pitted and chopped

½ cup/60 g crumbled feta cheese

½ cup/20 g finely grated Parmesan cheese

¼ teaspoon chili pepper flakes

2 eggs, lightly beaten

¼ cup/60 ml milk or sour cream

2 tablespoons olive oil

⅓ cup/45 g flour or cornstarch

1 tablespoon baking powder

½ teaspoon garlic powder

½ teaspoon salt

A few grindings of black pepper

Heat the oven to 350°F/180°C. Grease a 24-hole muffin tin, or use a non-stick pan.

Grate the zucchini on a box grater set on a clean tea towel. Gather the towel up in a ball, and squeeze out all the water over the sink. Shake the dry zucchini into a bowl and fork through the onion, basil, olives, feta, Parmesan, and chili pepper flakes.

Continued on the next page

Beat together the eggs, milk, and olive oil. Add the flour, baking powder, garlic powder, salt, and pepper. Mix well to combine, then stir into the zucchini mixture. Spoon the batter into the muffin tins.

Bake until puffed up and golden, 20 to 25 minutes. Remove from the oven, transfer to a platter, and serve warm or at room temperature.

Poached Leeks with Lemon Caper Dressing

What host doesn't relish the thought of a palate-awakening dish that's good in any season, easy to scale up for a crowd, and fine to prepare in advance? If all you can find are giant leeks, don't worry because you can always peel away some of the tougher outer leaves, once they're cooked, then cut lengthwise to serve each person a half. Be sure to take good care cleaning between the leaves at the top of the leek where sand can get trapped.

SERVES 4

4 medium-small leeks, trimmed and cleaned
Salt
2 small garlic cloves, grated
1 teaspoon Dijon mustard
2 tablespoons lemon juice
½ cup/125 ml olive oil
½ cup/20 g finely grated Parmesan cheese
2 tablespoons capers, chopped
A few pinches of thin lemon-peel strands, cut with a zester
Pepper
Fresh flat-leaf parsley leaves, for garnish

Bring a pan of water to a boil, large enough to hold the leeks lengthwise. Salt the water, then add the leeks and cook until tender, 10 to 15 minutes, depending on their size.

Whisk together the garlic, mustard, lemon juice, oil, Parmesan, and capers. Set aside.

Continued on the next page

When the leeks are done, drain and plunge into ice-cold water to stop the cooking. Remove and pat dry. Carefully halve lengthwise.

Arrange the leeks, cut side up, on a platter. Spoon over the dressing so it covers the entirety of the leeks. Scatter over the lemon zest, season with pepper, scatter over some roughly torn parsley leaves, and serve at room temperature.

36

In Praise of Boring Food

It's not uncommon to be reassured by cookbook authors that food isn't meant to be a performance, and that's a handy belief to cling to in moments of culinary stage fright. However, it's obviously not always true. I love the bold defiance of a restaurant like Next in Chicago, which literally runs itself like a theatre. Menus are created like musicals around a theme—Childhood, The Hunt, Paris 1906—and you more or less buy a ticket to attend the "show" during the limited time that it runs. I went to their vegan gastronomic performance a number of years ago and was positively dazzled. There were something like twenty-six courses, each with its own wine pairing, and each served on a unique serving dish designed specifically for the menu. The restaurant goes so far as to change props every time it changes theme, just like theatres change their sets for every new play. So, there's one example of food absolutely being about performance and unapologetically so.

Not long ago, my husband and I went to an abusively overpriced steakhouse where the food is entirely unsurprising—steak frites, lobster roll, crab cakes—and on a lark we ordered a tableside Caesar salad because, somehow, I'd managed to get that far in life without ever having seen it done. I rolled my eyes as the trolly carrying all the fixings was steered towards us, thinking, "How lame is this gimmick going to be?" Then, of course, I sat entranced as a young lad tilted a wooden bowl the size of a kitchen sink towards us and in it proceeded to mash together garlic, mustard, and anchovies, then add dashes of Worcestershire, tabasco, and a few other mystery ingredients, before piling in the lettuce, throwing in a feathery fistful of Parmesan cheese and another of golden croutons, then tossing the whole thing with the sort of gusto you'd expect from a juggler of flaming batons at the circus. I loved it, and the salad turned out to be one of the best Caesars I've ever tasted. How wonderful to have one's appetite for the unexpected stirred.

Tonight, we're going with a friend to her private club, and it's with great anticipation of an entirely different kind: total predictability. The menu there is also as unchanging as the Ten Commandments: oysters, jellied consommé, beef tartare, sole meunière. Like countless of its counterparts around the globe, it has leather chairs, white tablecloths, drinks first in the library by a roaring fire, dark wood-panelled walls, and a lot of men of a certain age in suits reminiscing about their glory days on Bay Street (Wall Street, the City . . .) and comparing golf handicaps. I'm looking forward to tonight precisely because I know exactly what to expect, which means if you ever hear me mock American tourists for going to McDonald's in Europe, you can call me a hypocrite and I'll be defenseless.

Or not, because, surely, it's the more adventurous eaters amongst us who ultimately get the most pleasure out of so-called "boring food." Yes, the epicure relishes exciting dining experiences and any chance to venture out of his comfort zone, but that's what makes his eventual return to the tried and true such a happy occasion. I had to laugh on my last visit home when my father offered, "How about cheesy peas on toast for lunch?" When's the last time I'd have had that, four decades ago? He went to the stove and boiled some peas, whipped up a béchamel and added loads of grated orange cheddar, then toasted some of his own oatmeal brown bread and plated it with a side of hot pickles before my devouring eyes. How marvellous when something totally familiar can at the same time have such power to surprise and delight.

Another completely boring dish that just about brought tears to my eyes recently was pâtes au beurre. It was Peter this time who made it, and I can't remember the occasion but there must have been one because he prepared it with an attention to detail he usually reserves for something like the annual Christmastime foie gras terrine. He even went to the trouble of adding a dash of truffle oil, and the whole thing (essentially buttered spaghetti with grated Parmesan cheese) suddenly seemed like a genius invention instead of the most banal bowl of pasta on the planet that it is.

The thing about boring food, a term I'm using to refer to food that we know like the back of our hands, is that it's never actually boring when it's truly good. Juicy, sun-ripened tomatoes, simply sliced and sprinkled with fleur de sel, are perfection. They don't even need olive oil. A proper baguette one can enjoy every day of life and never tire of. How about a warm bowl of oatmeal with brown sugar and farm-fresh cream? My mouth is watering . . .

I do love culinary fireworks as much as the next guy. In a few weeks, we'll be back in Paris and I say bring on the hay-smoked beets with trout eggs and Breton buttermilk, the miso-gratinéed leek with eel, the deconstructed mango cheesecake with crumbled meringue. I'll want it all and I'll never want it to end. Yes to the chicken bouillon with foie gras and grapefruit! Gimme that lamb tartare with "granola"! No, make that a langoustine in ginger nage! Until I will want it to end, of course. I'll hit that wall that makes me do something insane like cancel a coveted reservation at a three-star restaurant because I desperately need to stay in and eat cheesy rice from a bowl with a spoon.

As with all things in life we need balance. Sometimes we want to dance, sometimes we want to sit on a log by a river and think. Sometimes we want to put on a gown and sparkles, sometimes we want to hide under a blanket. Sometimes we crave a Next in Chicago where we might get edamame purée with edible flowers and I forget what else served on a rock or delicate mignardises arriving at the table on a chocolate Ferris wheel. And, sometimes we just want to be taken out to a leathery club where, exactly like last time, we can have the prawn cocktail, a couple of lamb chops with potato gratin, and a ball of vanilla ice cream. Boring. Utterly boring! You can tell me all about it. But, how wonderfully, magnificently, exquisitely boring when it's done right and is exactly what you need.

Fish Soup from Home

This is one of my mother's staple soups, now also one of mine, and a classic of Maritime cooking. I was once at a cocktail party in Nova Scotia where a pot of this was brought out just before people were leaving, so that they had something warm in their bellies before they hit the road, a sort of Maritime answer to pasta di mezzanotte. My mother refuses to serve this soup unless it has had at least one night in the fridge to mellow before reheating. It's even better on day three.

SERVES 4 TO 6

1 pound/450 g frozen haddock

2 cups/500 ml water, plus more as needed

1 onion, minced

4 large Yukon Gold potatoes (about 1½ pounds/675 g), peeled and diced

1 tin evaporated milk, 12 ounces/354 ml

Salt and pepper

Pinch of paprika

A large handful of finely chopped fresh flat-leaf parsley

2 tablespoons butter

Lay the fish, still frozen, in a large pot and pour the water over. Cover and place over medium-high heat until the fish thaws and flakes, only 3 to 5 minutes (don't overcook it). Remove the fish with a slotted spoon to a dish and set aside. Add the onion and potatoes to the fishy water, and, if necessary, top up so the potatoes are just covered with water. Bring to a simmer and gently cook until the vegetables are tender, about 15 minutes.

Break up the cooked fish and stir it into the soup, along with the milk. Season with salt, pepper, and paprika, then stir in the parsley and the butter. Remove from the heat. Cool, and refrigerate for a day or two before reheating to serve.

Polenta with Basil Oil

Not all food that one might consider boring has to be. This make-ahead polenta to slice for grilling or frying is highly seasoned and very flavourful, excellent as a side dish and, if you ask me, even good enough to serve as a first course, perhaps with some roasted cherry tomatoes or peppers alongside. For the basil oil, simply put a large handful of basil in the blender (blanched first in salted boiling water, if you'd like it electric green), and purée with just enough olive oil so that the mixture pours easily off a spoon.

SERVES 4

3½ cups/875 ml water
1½ teaspoons salt
1 cup/175 g polenta
2 tablespoons cream cheese or ricotta cheese
½ cup/20 g finely grated Parmesan
Freshly ground pepper
2 to 3 tablespoons basil oil (see headnote)

Put the water and salt in a large saucepan and bring to a boil. Lower the heat and add the polenta in a thin stream, whisking for a minute or two until the mixture has amalgamated. Now turn the heat to low, and let the mixture gently heave and sigh, uncovered, for about 35 minutes, stirring regularly with a wooden spoon until thick and soft.

Remove from the heat, stir in the cheeses and pepper until smooth, then ribbon the basil oil through the polenta. If you want to serve it straight away in this creamy state, go ahead, but otherwise pour it into a 9 × 5-inch/23 × 12-cm loaf pan lined with plastic wrap, and let set. Once firm, turn it onto a board and slice. Brush the slices with olive oil and fry until golden and heated through. Serve warm or at room temperature.

37

Grace Under Pressure

If you're looking for a "first world problem," I'd say having the city run out of Champagne for a few weeks during a pandemic would be worthy of a top-of-the-list position. First it was the shop up the street, which dwindled down to its last two bottles of Veuve, then it was the one at the foot of the hill, reduced one day to a single bottle of pink bubbly that had to be produced from the back of the store. It turned out to have been another instance of a whole supply being trapped on a ship, for whatever reason, no relation to the case of the entrepreneurial toilet-paper hoarder from COVID's early days, who thought he could make a fortune reselling it. Then there was the run on yeast, when everybody panicked in the first lockdown and suddenly took to therapeutic bread-making. Little setbacks, none of which lasted for very long, but which were enough to make at least some of us realize just how much we take for granted in this world.

I went through a phase that lasted several years when, every time

I took a shower, I found myself feeling awash with gratitude for the miracle of hot water. (I mean, just think how few people on the planet have experienced life with that luxury.) It was a powerful sensation that would cause me to shut my eyes and exhale with the sort of incredulous relief of one who'd just squeezed onto the last lifeboat of a sinking ship. "How is it possible that I'm so lucky?" I'd think to myself. There was another era of bonding with water that felt similar, and that was also during the pandemic because our friend Nona (to whom this book is dedicated) happened to have a forty-foot indoor pool (yes, I know that was even more ludicrously lucky), which she kept at roughly the temperature of a cup of tea, and I was allowed to use it. Hallelujah! Every time I'd descend the steps into that embracing aquamarine, the weight of the world would lift off my shoulders like a yoke. Some days, I actually said out loud the words, "Thank you, pool!" That first winter lockdown, it was the thing that saved my sanity.

I wonder when exactly saying grace—thanking some higher power for the meal at hand—went out of fashion. I myself was never a practitioner and, looking back, from my teenage years onwards anyway, I seldom witnessed it said in public. This was a relief, because for some reason it always made me uncomfortable, but now in the wisdom of oncoming old age, I wonder if there isn't something to it. I can't be alone, because despite grace having more or less gone the way of the dodo, "gratitude" has become one of the biggest buzzwords of the new century. Every self-help guru from here to Kingdom Come insists that nothing in life will go right without gratitude. Mind you, a few too many of them seem overly focused on using gratitude to manifest things like bigger cars and more money. I'm not sure quite how that works, because it sounds a lot more like "pretty please" than it does any "merci." Since when did gratitude become a demand?

The year I lived in Munich way back when, a family I knew used to say a little grace before every Mittagessen, and I can still remember it:

Erde, die uns dies gebracht
Sonne, die es reif gemacht
Liebe Sonne, liebe Erde,
Euer nie vergessen werde.

"Earth, who has brought us this/Sun who has ripened it/Dear Sun, Dear Earth/May you never be forgotten." Ah, now that may explain something, because have we not largely forgotten? Have we not been so long spoiled by an uninterrupted supply of food—not to mention clothes, gadgets, heat, light, and freedom—that we've come to believe they're all our God-given right? It's possible that we can't truly learn to be grateful by having things given to us, but only by having them taken away. "Absence makes the heart grow fonder," as those of us who were separated by COVID from family for well on two years found out.

"We do not presume to come to this thy table, O merciful Lord, trusting in our own righteousness, but in thy manifold and great mercies. We are not worthy so much as to gather up the crumbs under thy table . . ."

That's the beginning of the Anglican Church's Prayer of Humble Access, which has just sprung into my head like some long-forgotten pop song. I'd have repeated those lines countless times in my youth, though never paid attention to their meaning at the time. Looking at them now, I see there is an essential link between gratitude and humility. Food is life, the manna which sustains us, without which we would succumb. How dare we tear it off the shelves and gulp it down our throats without any acknowledgement of that fact, nor with any recognition that whenever we do we've taken another life, whether it be pig, parsley, or peanut, to keep our own going? Euer nie vergessen werde.

I remember going to lunch once during university with a young Jewish lad who disappeared to wash his hands before he would touch his food, and also quietly said a prayer before eating. He didn't go into any great explanation about it, but I remember he gave me a heads-up, "Excuse me. I just have to do a few things." I found it curious at the time, but now I wonder if he wasn't on to something. Remember all those experiments on ice crystals a few decades ago in Japan that showed how they're affected by words and music, contracting into ugly blobs at the sound of harshness and discord and expanding into glorious, snowflake-shaped jewels to sounds beautiful and harmonious? Food is mostly made up of water. As are we.

Clearly this is not my area of expertise, but this is where ignorance truly can be bliss: it keeps a mind open and receptive. Well, I'm certainly receptive to the idea that any of us with the good fortune to share good food with good people every day—to be reminded we exist, to be nourished, warmed, fed ideas and made to laugh, reassured we belong and have a place in this world—we are lucky beyond belief. The medieval German theologian Meister Eckhart said, "If the only prayer you ever say in your entire life is thank you, it will be enough."

Amen to that.

And à table!

Fennel and Rosemary Breadsticks

We tend to think of bread-making as an involved project, but the actual hands-on work here is minimal and quick, well worth it for fragrant, crisp, hot breadsticks straight from the oven. Addictive. These are also good made with 2 tablespoons of toasted sesame seeds instead of fennel and rosemary.

MAKES ABOUT 40

⅔ cup/150 ml lukewarm water

1 teaspoon sugar

1 package yeast (2¼ teaspoons)

2 tablespoons olive oil

2 cups/250 g bread flour

1½ teaspoons salt

1 tablespoon fennel seed, slightly crushed, or sesame seeds

1 tablespoon chopped fresh rosemary leaves

Fleur de sel, for garnish

Stir together the water, sugar, and yeast in the bowl of a stand mixer with hook attachment, and let sit for 5 minutes until foamy. Add the oil, flour, salt, fennel seed, and rosemary and mix on medium low, scraping the sides of a bowl with a spatula a couple of times near the beginning, for 10 minutes. Cover the resulting dough with a clean tea towel and let rise to double, about an hour.

Punch down the dough, roll it flat into a square, and cut into 40 pieces. Roll each out into a very thin stick, 10 to 12 inches long, giving a final roll in a sprinkling of fleur de sel, and lay the breadsticks on a parchment-lined baking sheet. Let rest for 15 minutes while you heat the oven to 425°F/220°C. Bake, in batches if necessary, until the sticks are golden, and crisp enough to snap in two, about 15 minutes.

Mum's Bread Rolls

These delicious milk-rich rolls have always been a family staple for serving with soups and also for making lunchtime sandwiches, such as roast beef and horseradish or cheddar and lettuce. They travel well.

MAKES 24 TO 30

2 cups/500 ml milk

¼ cup/60 g butter

¼ cup/60 g to ½ cup/100 g sugar

1 teaspoon salt

1 package yeast (2¼ teaspoons)

½ cup/125 ml warm water

6 cups/750 g flour, plus more as needed

2 tablespoons melted butter, for rolling and brushing

Heat the milk and butter in a saucepan until the butter has melted. Remove from the heat and stir in the sugar and salt. Pour into a large mixing bowl and set aside to cool until tepid.

Dissolve the yeast in the warm water and let sit for about 5 minutes until foamy, then stir into the cooled milk mixture. (Make sure it's not hot or you could kill the yeast, which will prevent the dough from rising.) Stir in half the flour, then mix in the rest. The dough should be quite sticky, but not unmanageably so. If it is, you can add another handful of flour so that the dough pulls shaggily away from the side of the bowl. (You are not looking for a smooth dough that forms a ball. That would mean you've added too much flour and the rolls will be heavy.)

Put the dough in a clean bowl, cover with a tea towel, set in a warm place, and let rise to double, 1 to 1½ hours. Punch the dough down, cover again, and let rise to double a second time, about 30 minutes. Grease 2 large baking sheets. Heat the oven to 350°F/180°C.

Have the melted butter in a small bowl by your side. Dip your fingers into the butter and tear a piece of dough from the mass, about 2 ounces/60 g. Shape into a ball and set on one of the baking sheets. Continue making balls this way and arranging them on the sheets, spaced slightly apart. Brush the tops with melted butter. Let rise to double yet again, about 30 minutes, then bake, one pan at a time, until fully cooked through and golden, 18 to 20 minutes.

Afterword

What Is Your Kitchen Bliss?

. . . making tea in the early morning hours
when you're the first one up

. . . coming home to the scent of onions frying in butter

. . . finding an I ♥ YOU note stuck to the fridge door with a magnet

. . . chopping vegetables with a newly sharpened knife

. . . watching broth bubble through a raft and
go from cloudy to amber clear

. . . a table surrounded by friends who think you're the cat's meow

. . . Saturday morning at the market on a sunny day

. . . rosé at lunchtime

. . . finding a recipe of your grandmother's
that you thought you'd lost

. . . hearing the gentle slap of a screen door
leading in from the garden

. . . reorganizing a spice shelf and putting fresh labels on all the tins

. . . making a tricky dish for the first time and having it work out

. . . discovering there's just enough mayonnaise
left in the jar for your egg sandwich

. . . finding the first ripe cherry tomato in the window box

. . . a new set of dinner plates

Recipes by Course

FIRST COURSES AND SALADS

MAIN DISHES

SIDE DISHES

DESSERTS

Acknowledgements

This book exists because I was given the generous freedom by my editor, Kirsten Hanson, to write "a food narrative with recipes." Carte blanche! There were many twists and turns from start to finish, but I'm happy where it ended up. Thank you, Kirsten—and Simon & Schuster Canada—for putting your trust in me, and for your patient and sensitive guidance throughout the journey.

I extend huge thanks to my agent, Grainne Fox at Fletcher & Co., for pushing me to take full charge of my voice with this book, and to make the most of the project. Thank you also, Grainne, for getting this project into the right hands, and for your constant, steady support over the years.

I am grateful to a number of people who took the time, in the final stages, to read my manuscript and share their valuable feedback. My parents, John and Doris Calder; my husband, Peter Scowen; and my friend Bridget Colman all had a hand in polishing the text—and keeping me out of hot water! I also thank Tudor Alexis for his vetting of my pieces related to India and diplomacy.

Thank you to copy editor Janet McDonald for fine-tuning the manuscript with such painstaking care. A big thank you to designer Paul Barker for his blissful cover design, and especially for his patience with all the back and forth that inevitably goes into pleasing so many stakeholders. And thank you to my friend Bill Hutchison for scanning my "doodles," and for encouraging me to do them in the first place.

It takes a village, as they say. I count my lucky stars for the one I had around me throughout the creation of *Kitchen Bliss: Musings on Food and Happiness (With Recipes)*.